TAKE A BIG BITE

Although this old photograph looks like Lee, it's actually a photo of President Ulysses S. Grant.

Take a big bite!

Moderation is for monks.
Specialization is for insects.

Events and people in the life of

Lee Lynch

Tasora

Take A Big Bite:
Moderation is for monks. Specialization is for insects.

Edited by Terry Saario and Rosanne Monten
Designed by Michael Skjei

ISBN 978-1-948192-19-4
Printed in Minneapolis, Minnesota at Shapco Printing
First Printing: 2021

Tasora Books
5120 Cedar Lake Road
Minneapolis, MN 55416
(952) 345-4488
Distributed by Itasca Books

ALSO BY THE AUTHOR:

Amazing MN*: State Rankings & Unusual Information, 2017*

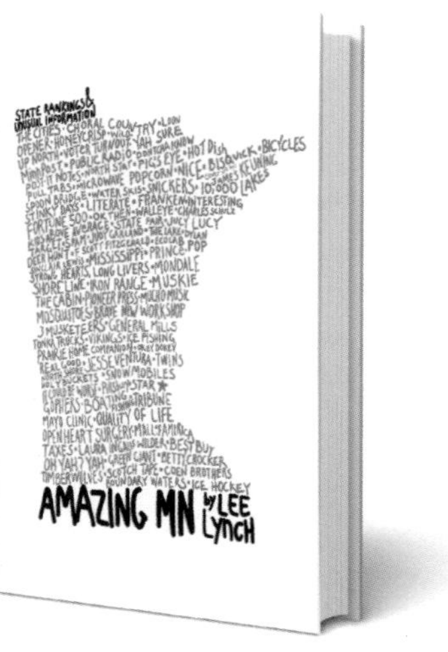

This book is dedicated to Rosanne Monten who for over fifty years has been my scheduler, organizer, adviser, banker, accountant, pay master, apologist, editor, fact checker and dear friend. She has tolerated my foibles and failures without a harsh word or even a lifted eyebrow. She made me laugh and smile every day AND *is overjoyed that this damn book is finally done.*

x *Introduction*
1 *Anderson Drugstore*
4 *Education in Belle Plaine*
7 *Priests in my Life*
10 *Band of Brothers*
12 *Military Me*
15 *Frog Gigging*
17 *The Star Tribune Effect*
20 *Camilo Pascual*
22 *Workspace*
26 *Manufacturing Fun*
31 *John Marks*
34 *A Tremor in the Blood*
37 *The Great Sign Theft*
40 *Long Hairs Only*
44 *Kenny O*
46 *Grey, Gray, Grey*
48 *Financial Advice*
51 *A Memorable Wedding*
53 *A Pair of Singles*
55 *Neal Cheney*
57 *The O'Gong Show*
59 *Minnesota Fats*
64 *Civic Actions*
67 *Jack, Always Creative*
69 *Courtship of Terry*
71 *Mess'n with Terry*
73 *Power Couple*
75 *Brother Tommy*
78 *Tom Lynch in Ireland*
81 *Surprising Tom and Ethel*
83 *Some Remembrances of T.H.*
87 *Sorta Claus*
89 *Head in the Game*
91 *Edgar*
94 *Death and Dying*
98 *Birthday Surprises*
103 *Lonnie*
105 *Maury Hurley*
109 *Heavy Metal*
111 *Dinner with the Boys*
113 *Joe and Rose*
115 *Chieu*
119 *Wrong Place, Wrong Time*
122 *Some Bad Days*
125 *Arne Carlson*
127 *Walter Mondale*
129 *Graves vs. Bachmann*
132 *Boring Commencement Speech?*
134 *Boys' Night Out*
137 *Las Palomas*
140 *Musical Highlights*
143 *Reykjavik*
146 *Famous Names*
150 *My Body is a Temple*
153 *Unusual Funerals*
157 *Helicopter Skiing Caper*
160 *Law, Order and David Lykken*

162 *Officer Gene Manly*
164 *The Perfect Pitch*
166 *Wild Blue Yonder*
170 *The Sumpter Family of Kentucky*
172 *The Mall of America*
175 *Maestro of Minnesota*
177 *Fritz*
179 *Fartburg*
181 *Evelyn's Ashes*
184 *World Leaders Tour*
186 *Don't Cry For Me*
189 *Belize*
192 *David of Cape Town*
195 *Chinese Medicine*
197 *Turkish Bath*
200 *Tight Spaces*
203 *Stunning Sites*
205 *Liverpool*
207 *Japan Man*
210 *Going Down the Yukon*
214 *Greatest Trip*
218 *El Gaucho Gordo*
220 *Ephesus*
221 *Dogon Country*
223 *Asleep in Finland*
226 *River Nose*
229 *Swedish Olympics*
231 *Siberian Sprint*
235 *Obituary*

Take a Big Bite!

Moderation is for monks.

Specialization is for insects.

These phrases were taken from a book by Robert Heinlein, *Time Enough for Love.*

My friends and my wife Terry concur that I took a big bite out of life and am neither moderate in anything I do nor am I specialized. People say I am excessive–a mile wide and one inch deep.
But entertaining!

I wrote these stories because that's what old men do...write stories about their lives.

This collection represents the most unusual events and people in my life. These are all true stories. I changed names and locations in three of them so I would not embarrass anyone or get sued.

I expect my children and grandchildren will enjoy this book. I hope you will find a few of the stories of interest. Think about writing your own.

LEE LYNCH
Entrepreneur, Writer, Lover, Citizen

Everyone should have a color.

TAKE A BIG BITE

ANDERSON DRUGSTORE

Sex Education On The Job

I ALWAYS HAD A JOB WHEN I WAS A KID. I sold popcorn at the town baseball games and made a lot on tips. I was just too cute with my little sailor hat. On Wednesday and Saturday nights, Pork Chop Hagerman and I towed our shoeshine stand up the street and parked it directly across from the portable bandstand. Farmers came to town to shop, drink and listen to a bad band composed of some high schoolers and a few community members who had lost their "lips." We split 50/50 and that was enough to keep me in as much grape soda as I could drink. I never told my parents how much we earned. They would have wanted me to save it for a rainy day.

When not in school I read comics at the drugstore. My literary IQ started and finished with Classic Comics. I liked *Les Mis.* I would become so absorbed in the comics I wouldn't hear a thing including Mr. Thompton telling me the store was closing. One evening my dad and Mr. Thompton played a trick on me. They turned off the lights, locked the doors and spied on me to see what I would do when I realized I was locked in. I panicked. Bad trick.

When I entered seventh grade, Mr. Thompton asked if I wanted a job sweeping out the drugstore and being a stock boy. I was excited. A real job with a weekly paycheck. I soon found out Kotex napkins were not dinner napkins. I waited on customers after two years. Eventually if there weren't after-school practices, I clerked after school and every Saturday all day until 9 p.m. and Sunday morning from 9 to noon. When I was a senior in high school, I frequently violated the law by filling some simple prescriptions because Mr. Anderson (the new owner) didn't like coming in on Sunday mornings.

I was the envy of my pals when I was a high school junior and senior. I was behind the counter with some of the hotties in town. Leona Mueller (26), Mary Johnson (21) and Eunice O'Brien (18). They were all attractive. Leona was the topic of most inquiries. She was about five-feet tall and petite except for a 42D cup bosom. Men of all ages would come to gawk, especially my buddies. They all wanted to know if I ever brushed against them (they were always called "them"). They were envious of my familiarity with Leona especially when I told them I could snap her bra strap (which I never did). My four buddies each bet me a dollar to snap her bra strap in front of them without Leona getting upset. I took the bet. I told Leona about the bet and offered her half if she would smile after I snapped her bra. My friends came in the next Saturday and stood by the newsstand. Bets on. I waved Leona to come over, winked at her and snapped her bra strap. She slapped my face. I lost $4. Never trust a woman.

On a Saturday night between my freshman and sophomore year I waited on a hog farmer named Cletus Pilgrim. In previous trips to the store he always went to the back of the store and quietly talked to the pharmacist. But on this night Mr. Anderson wasn't in the store so Mr. Pilgrim came up to me and in a whisper asked for a dozen skins. I had no idea what he was talking about so I hollered out to Leona who was at the other end of a very crowded store, "Leona, where do we keep the skins?"

Cletus never came back. I wondered what he did with a dozen skins every two weeks. His wife did look tired all the time. Was it possible?

Eunice was embarrassed to discuss it. Leona said she would not mind getting "it" six times a week. Mary thought it was about pigs.

My sex education continued with the help of Leona, Eunice, Mary, Trojans, Skins, Tampax and of course, Mr. Anderson. He enjoyed telling me slightly off-color stories.

Downtown Belle Plaine. Anderson Drugstore was in the middle of the block.

Belle Plaine's claim to fame, a two-story outhouse.

EDUCATION IN BELLE PLAINE

Age 5 to 17, A Good Deal

I NEVER FELT I GOT A GOOD EDUCATION. Mostly my fault but not entirely.

GRADE SCHOOL

I got off to a bad start in my small class (there were only six of us) at Sacred Heart School, the Irish school. The population was declining and financing diminishing. They decided to close the school.

We were marched six blocks to the German school where the nuns were all from Germany and had heavy accents, Sisters Alfleada, Hildegard, Luke and Austrian. All the Irish had to sit at the back of the classroom. One day the whole class prayed for my mother's conversion to Catholicism.

I went through the eighth grade at St. Peter and Paul's learning a lot about sin and funerals. The entire school was dismissed to sing at every funeral. There were about two a week.

My understanding of sin came through milk bottles. Black for mortal, gray for venial and white for no sin. To this day I don't drink milk.

The nuns taught us about ejaculations...short prayers directly to God, used only in an emergency. I told some of the older guys in the eighth grade about ejaculations. They all laughed. I didn't know what was so funny.

The library on the second floor was in a closet lined with shelves of old books. No one can remember ever taking a book out of the library.

I remember a lot of art, large friezes on butcher paper. I had to fill in the colors between the lines because I couldn't draw. I don't remember much about math or non-religious literature. I did like the Crusades in the sixth grade. There goes religion again.

I was well drilled in catechism. I appeared on a radio quiz show every Sunday morning called *Catechism Comes to Life* with Father Gayles, a well know anti-communist. I lasted four weeks until some smart city girl aced me out. My parents were proud. I'm not sure I kept winning because of my answers or because I sounded convincing with a loud and resolute answer.

St. Peter and Paul's was convenient to our apartment over the general store, only one block away. I had to walk by Ed Moody's chicken business where he candled eggs and butchered chickens. Yucky smell. I also had to walk past old Mr. Reynolds who sat on his porch yelling he was going to cut off the ears of the kids who passed by.

HIGH SCHOOL

High school was a sad awakening. The quality of our Catholic education was abysmal. I took algebra along with three of my Catholic buddies. We failed all six report cards. A whole year of straight Fs in math. Little did I know that doomed any chance of finishing in the top ten in my class. I took algebra again the next year and aced it. Too little, too late.

I liked moving from room to room and seeing all the students from the public schools as well as some from farm schools.

I loved band and the poor disabled instructor, Fran Richards. A large hump in his back made it hard for him to keep up with the marching band. We were a very slow marching band. I had no choice of instrument and was assigned tenor sax because the sax player was graduating.

I played basketball and baseball. Freshmen weren't allowed to play football. All these activities plus my twenty hours a week job at the drugstore made me a busy boy with no time or, it seemed, need to study. My parents were not concerned.

I went steady with Mary Trimbo from my junior year on. I was sure I would marry her but after one quarter at the University of Minnesota we both went our ways.

My high school was small. My class had only 60 students. I had to play all three sports to help fill out the teams. Belle Plaine did not have a hockey team, track team or even a swimming pool. We had so few football players on the team that we didn't have enough for a scrimmage. Alumni were invited to come out and kill us. They loved reliving their athletic careers.

I was in glee club, junior and senior class plays, and oratory. It was oratory and Miss Lang who gave me my greatest success. I was the only person to win State competition twice…once for dramatic reading in my junior year and once for original oratory in my senior year. I traveled all over the state to enter competitions with Miss Lang and became quite fond of her. She was about 23 and maybe too fond of me. Nothing happened. Belle Plaine had not paid its dues to the National Forensic League so I could not advance to the nationals. My dad was furious!

I loved high school, lived life to the fullest, didn't smoke or drink, didn't study and did well on the ACTs. I was off to the University of Minnesota.

Looking back I now realize how lucky I was to be born into a loving family, in a small age cohort (due to the Depression), in a typical small town, with a small high school, in a progressive state and a great country.

Hooray for Belle Plaine.

THE PRIESTS IN MY LIFE

Why I Wandered

I WAS RAISED CATHOLIC, IRISH CATHOLIC rather than German Catholic. There were two Catholic churches in Belle Plaine and two more Catholic churches nearby, one three miles north and the other three miles south of town. There were five other denominations in Belle Plaine including Presbyterian, my mother's church. They were, as they said, non-Catholic.

I was the product of a scandalous marriage. Tom Lynch the barber, son of the blacksmith, married the daughter of the town merchant and Gustavus Adolphus graduate. They said the marriage would never last but it did for 69 loving years.

Every new priest to Sacred Heart Parish would visit my mother and try to convert her. She hated them for trying. One even tried to convert her as she was dying. She told my wife Terry, "They were here, the priests, tell them not to come back."

I vaguely recall cherubic Father Minouge from Ireland but I do remember Father Miller, the German priest. His real last name was Benveneute but that must have been too hard for the parish to remember. Father Miller would come into class, lead a prayer and bless all of us. The nun would then ask all the boys who would like to be a priest to stand up. We all stood in the first and second grades. A few of us didn't stand as we moved into the third and fourth grades. Even less stood in the fifth and sixth-grade classrooms. Only Roger Hessian stood up in the seventh and eighth grades and he was swept away to the seminary in St. Paul.

I was an altar boy at Sacred Heart for only a few months. I hated getting up at 6 a.m. for early daily mass and I didn't like the priest, Father Finlay. He was mean, very old and made a constant slurping sound. Father Finlay frequently chewed out Tommy Hessian (Roger's cousin) and me. To retaliate Tommy peed in the sacramental wine without Father knowing it. It was hard not to laugh as he drank the salty wine while slurping loudly. Tommy was also snatched up and sent to the seminary but he failed out. He liked girls.

Every year a new young priest fresh out of seminary was assigned as an assistant to Father Finlay. I remember father Rowan, Father Westphal and above all Father Murphy (who went on to become the president of University of St. Thomas in St. Paul). Later in life, I learned that Father Finlay was a huge problem for the Archbishop. His colleagues called him Bingo Bill. No one could take more than a year of Bingo Bill. I heard he ended up in a home for alcoholic priests.

My nemesis was Father O'Conner. He taught religion to we "catlicks" once a week in the Knights of Columbus hall located above Curley's bar. I loathed going there with a passion. O'Conner hated anyone questioning the faith and came down hard on me for asking obvious questions. That's when I became a non-believer and faked my religion from then on. He was a tyrant.

While in grade school I had a classmate for a short time named George Schroeder. George lived near me and we played together. George liked to sing and dress up as a priest. He too went into the seminary at the seventh grade. We reunited years later. George was a good guy, an exciting preacher, pastor and singer. George went on to become a monsignor in the Denver Archdiocese. I hope to see him someday.

At the University of Minnesota I was exposed to my first urbane, sophisticated priest, Father George Garraults. He was cool and headed the campus Newman Center. Everyone was disappointed when he ran off and got married.

My former wife Mary's old parish priest in St. Paul wanted to meet me before he officiated at our wedding. The meeting didn't go well and he told the Martin family that perhaps I was not a good match. I can't remember what question tripped me up, probably the one about Lazarus being raised from the dead or the immaculate conception.

I tried religion once again after we had kids. We joined Visitation Church which also ran a school. I sang folk songs with a friend Steve Johnson, the guitar player. That didn't last long. We migrated to a very liberal parish, St. Joan of Arc, led by Father Harvey Egan. Harvey was a piece of work and became a good friend. As a member of the parish council, I had to go to the Archbishop's office and defend Harvey for being too contemporary. Sunday mass at St. Joan's was an uplifting experience. We prayed to God our Mother and listened to Gloria Steinem, Cesar Chavez, and Gene McCarthy while singing joyous Dylan, Beatles and Mamas and Papas songs.

St. Joan's was considered the last stop for Catholics and became the fastest-growing parish in five states. This troubled the Archbishop and he kept pressure on Harvey to conform or be sent to the boondocks until retirement. Harvey ended his priestly career in Albertville, Minnesota.

Years later, Terrance Murphy, then president of the University of St. Thomas, called. He wanted to visit me in my office. Thinking it was a solicitation, I asked him how much he wanted and for what. He excitedly said that he had something to give to me. He came to the office. He started his presentation noting that he and I went way back to Belle Plaine where he gave me my first communion. Then he disclosed his gift, an invitation to join the board of directors of the *Catholic Digest* (as he placed multiple copies of it on my desk). He was beaming. I asked if he knew I was on the Planned Parenthood board of directors. Father Murphy's face fell as he scooped up the copies of the *Digest* and departed without even saying goodbye. I never heard from him again.

Α Β Γ Δ Ε Ζ

Η Θ Ι Κ Λ Μ Ν

Ξ Ο Π Ρ Σ Τ Υ

Φ Χ Ψ Ω

BAND OF BROTHERS

They Did Well

My sister Karen insisted that I join a fraternity at the U of M. She also insisted that it be Chi Psi as she knew some of the members and thought they were a decent group as opposed to members of the party palaces. As president of the 8,000-freshman class, I was a desirable prospect and was pledged immediately. She had me get rid of my Belle Plaine clothes and buy a charcoal gray blazer, rep tie and button-down shirt. I can't thank her enough for that sartorial advice.

Over the next four years, I got to know several fellow members. Some were serious students (not many) and some were strictly party boys. About 60% lived in the metro area and commuted to campus. The rest were from small towns and other cities.

My years at the University were marked by my extraordinary investment in extra-curricular activities. Freshman class president, debate team, chair of Welcome Week (paid position), new student orientation sponsor (also paid), fraternity president for 18 months (free room and board), All U Congress and a run at student body president. (I was killed in the election. Frat boys were not popular with the main student body.) I also worked every day at the *Star Tribune* newspaper as a tour guide and copy boy. If there had been a major in leadership at the university I would have graduated summa cum laude.

I was not active in the fraternity alumni association until I was invited to be the guest speaker at one of their annual alumni dinners. I became reacquainted with some of my old "brothers."

I recently started to think about the successful lives of some of my brothers (class of 1954–58). I don't know if it's unusual or common but a significant number of leaders were in that class:

–ARNE CARLSON *became Governor of Minnesota.*

–DENNY SANFORD *(my former wife's old boyfriend) became a billionaire and donated $450 million to a health clinic in South Dakota.*

–LONNIE HAMMERGREN *became a psychiatrist and then Lieutenant Governor of Nevada.*

–BILL PEDERSON *became head of one of the nation's hottest architectural firms based in* NYC.

–JOHN CUNINGHAM *became a leading architect with offices in Minneapolis and Asia.*

–SARGE KYLE *became a prominent federal judge.*

–*Four doctors, a dentist, an Army general, and three professors.*

–*An Episcopal priest, and some lawyers.*

–*And an ad guy, me.*

Looking back, my brothers were an interesting group. They were all gentlemen. I benefited from their friendship.

I couldn't believe I was drafted into the peacetime Army. Why me?

MILITARY ME

Don't Get In My Foxhole

I WAS DRAFTED INTO THE US ARMY in March 1960. Drafted! No one was drafted. There were just so many ways to beat the draft. But I got nailed. I did not qualify as a full-time student taking only nine graduate credits. Teaching at the Home of the Good Shepherd part-time did not grant me a teaching deferment.

I wasn't worried. I had a very slow heartbeat. My friend Andy Kenyon's father was a doctor and wrote to the draft board that he was concerned about my "slow" heart. Bradycardia they called it. The draft board wasn't buying it.

My wife, Mary, drove me to the federal building four times. Three times I failed the heart test. They nailed me on the fourth. My heart rate quickened with the prospect of shipping out that morning.

The next thing I knew I was on a train to Camp Carson, Colorado. A greasy longhaired 18-year-old sat down beside me and said, "Hey buddy, the judge gave me the Army or jail. I chose the Army."

Three days earlier I had been teaching delinquent girls and now I was a "buddy" with a teenage delinquent boy.

I was shorn and tested at Camp Carson and immediately sent to Fort Hood for basic training. The first physical test at basic was easy for me to pass. I was in great shape except for pull-ups. The sergeant watching the bar became distracted and turned away as I approached the chin-up bar. I ran under the bar without touching it. I passed the physical with flying colors. I didn't have to do early morning physical training for the rest of my Army career.

They gave me an M1 rifle and taught me how to clean it. Before I even fired it once I was pulled into the commander's office to replace the sick company clerk. I could type 60 wpm. Three weeks later I was sent to code school at Fort Hood, Kentucky and for ten weeks played with all kinds of radios and code machines. I learned to send and receive 21 words per minute in Morse code. That speed and training gave me a special military occupational specialty (MOS) making me an acting Sgt. E-5. Real stripes even. The teaching experience at home qualified me to teach in the code school so I was never sent to a permanent company. I became a real Sgt. E-5 after only eight months in the Army, faster than Elvis Presley's record of nine months and I couldn't even sing!

I was offered the opportunity to go to Officer's Candidate School to serve three years in the mud of Germany or I could stay at Sgt. E-5 rank and remain in Kentucky at the same pay as a second lieutenant. Not a difficult choice. I was made an information non-com and taught current events to thousands of totally uninformed enlisted men. They were required to go to class once a week to stay informed about daily world events.

As an E-5 I could live off post with my wife. I found an idyllic place high up on the banks of the Ohio River near Brandenburg, Kentucky.

I taught in the mornings and played volleyball every afternoon. A year of competitive volleyball got me on the division team so I didn't have to teach in the mornings. I was a protected jock. My only other duty was to coach the regiment's basketball team. As coach I frequently put myself into play with college stars and future NBA star and coach Lennie Wilkins. They would never pass the ball to me. Damn.

I was up for an "early out," a practice in the peacetime Army. A flare-up with Russia in Berlin, "the Berlin Crisis," resulted in a four-month extension on my service because of my unique MOS.

At this point I didn't have to go to the Fort except to collect my check. I picked up a job in a drugstore in Valley Station, Kentucky while waiting for my extension to lapse. Then another surprise. Orders to go to Vietnam.

I had never fired a rifle and yet was going to be sent to a foreign country supposedly to set up information commands in small hamlets in South Vietnam. I would be an advisor because in 1962 we weren't formally at war.

Thirteen of us with communications ratings began to take classes on the history and culture of Vietnam. I started to panic. Mary was now pregnant and in Minneapolis. I was supposed to get a family discharge but the paperwork was lost. They started giving us vaccinations. I tried to avoid them by telling them I wasn't going to ship out. The others under the same orders knew I was not trained in any aspect of warfare and joked about how they didn't want me to be in their foxhole.

Finally, my dad called Jim Daly, an attorney in Belle Plaine, who called Senator Humphrey's office to clear up the paperwork log jam.

It worked. I was discharged and sent home. Years later Terry and I went to the Vietnam Memorial Wall in Washington, DC. There, on the wall, were the names of six or seven of my team members. I was stunned.

Later I ran across a report about the Strategic Hamlet Defense program. It didn't work, especially in the early years, when most of the communication advisors were killed.

Looking back, my time in the Army was a great experience. Volleyball, going to eastern Kentucky on weekends to learn about Appalachia and good times with new friends. Once again, I lucked out.

FROG GIGGING

Make Sure They Are Dead

I HAD AN EASY LIFE IN THE ARMY, living in an enchanted forest in rural Kentucky.

I was a Sgt. E-5 and living off post (Fort Knox) in a rustic, remote cabin on a 700-foot ledge overlooking the Ohio River right at the bend between Indiana and Kentucky. Because I knew Morse code I was able to communicate at night with the large barges on the river.

Another cabin nearby was occupied by a fellow GI. The people who owned the cabins, retired Chicago architects trying to escape from the world, lived near me. They were the original hippies, vegetarians and animal lovers.

I drove into Fort Knox every day and had to drive by a small Baptist church on a seldom-traveled road. I remember a large banner often hung on the church wall. "Beware of the Three C's: Catholics, Communists and Coloreds." I was deep in the heart of the old South. The nearest town, Brandenburg, was located on the banks of the river with only a rope barge powered by horses to cross to Indiana.

One day John Edstrom, the occupant of the other cabin, suggested we go frog gigging that night. I had no idea what frog gigging was but I was up for it. He was a Southern boy and loved to gig.

He gave me a long bamboo fishing pole with a barbed spear on the end and a small flashlight taped close to its end.

In the dead of night the two of us waded waist-high into a stinky swamp alive with bugs, snakes and hopefully frogs. We each carried a bag to put our catch in and started shining our larger flashlights around the banks looking for the reflection of frog eyes. When we spotted one we would get the barbed spear close to the frog and then make a quick impaling jab.

After an hour of terror (we were worried about snakes), we headed back to our cabins to fry the frogs and have a few beers. We killed the frogs by hitting them sharply on the head and cutting off their legs with scissors, throwing the body into the trash can. The legs were delicious.

I awoke the next morning to the owner's wife scream. She was beside herself and screaming like crazy. I went to the door to see why she was upset. The frogs were not dead, just missing their legs. The small garbage can had been overturned in the middle of the night. The legless torsos were dragging themselves onto the porch leaving a trail of oozing guts and blood. No wonder she was upset. Even I felt bad. Poor frogs. No more gigging for me.

THE STAR TRIBUNE EFFECT

A Long Thread

I WAS LUCKY AS AN UNDERGRADUATE to have a job as a tour guide at the *Star Tribune*. I was hired because I had won several state speech events and the job needed a "talker."

I was assigned to a desk in the promotion department when I was not leading tours. My job there was the mindless task of measuring all the self-promotion ads the paper ran. The management of the paper must have wanted those statistics for tax reasons. I got to know some of the writers in the department and watched what they wrote. I secretly compared what I would write on the same assignment to what they wrote. One of the writers who befriended me was Peter Georgas who wrote most of the promotional ads for various upcoming events. Peter arranged for my name to appear in the Sunday weekly crossword puzzle. That was cool.

I also met Jack Carmichael, a production artist in charge of the rotogravure section, at a chess tourney sponsored by the paper. Jack and I would hide out in the projection booth and play chess.

I worked at the paper for four years and did some occasional weekend copy boy assignments. I met many of the news writers and was impressed with how hard they worked and how grumpy they were–at least to me. I liked what they did and wished I had taken more journalism classes.

After graduation I was drafted by the US Army. I was teaching and taking graduate credits part time and became eligible for the draft. Woe was me.

The day I finally returned to the Twin Cities I called Jack. He had left the paper and was now a freelance art director.

I visited Jack in his basement workshop in his Brooklyn Center home. He had been counting on a writer to help him with a brochure. The writer took another job and Jack was stranded.

Jack knew the subject matter but could not write a word. He talked me through the project. I ended up writing the brochure and presenting it to the owner of a small metalworking company. He liked it and hired us to do a brochure for another machine.

I was hooked. I missed my interview at General Mills. Jack got another assignment. We became a team, Carmichael Lynch.

Even though Jack was an artist, he couldn't draw and hired freelance illustrators, usually another *Star Tribune* alum. Dave Van Giesen, "Goose" was the most frequent and we hired him.

Soon we needed a real writer and convinced Peter Georgas to leave the *Star Tribune* and join us as a partner. Then came Connie Razidlo. I knew him before I went into the Army. Connie had moved to New Mexico to sell ads for the local daily paper. I found out he was unhappy there so I lured him back over the phone by promising to pay his $400 moving costs.

Over the years these original partners went their separate ways but the thread to the *Star Tribune* remained. I hired a former sales manager for the paper, Lou Bacig, to be an account leader at the agency. Lou ended up becoming my friend and equal partner.

Years later Terry joined the board of Cowles Media, once headed by John Cowles, son of the founder of the *Star Tribune*. Over time we got to know John and his wife Sage and held them in high esteem.

I had good relations with the Cowles, George and Sally Pillsbury, Jim Binger and other pillars of the city. Connie once described me as a guy who went from no money to new money to old money–in one lifetime. Connie didn't really know what old money was but I loved his description.

I remain fond of the *Star Tribune* and journalism.

Laurie and Joel Kramer, the former CEO and publisher of the *Star Tribune*, John and Sage Cowles, David and Vicki Cox and Terry and I founded and financed the creation of one of the first daily online newspapers in the country, *MinnPost*. Our gift of $250,000 made me chairman and later chairman emeritus.

A part of my life was a significant 50-year thread with a wonderful company.

Camilo Pascual played for the Minnesota Twins from 1961 to 1971. He was inducted into the Twins Hall of Fame in 2012.

CAMILO PASCUAL

Breakthrough Creative

MY PARTNER JACK CARMICHAEL and I were getting tired of doing logos, brochures and the occasional car dealer radio spot.

Then a big opportunity. A new car dealer, Dick Lewis of Southtown Chrysler Plymouth, called to find out if we could do a TV spot to celebrate the first anniversary of his dealership.

We developed scores of ideas and presented the three best to Dick. All three required production costs. Dick said he wouldn't pay production. Get the station to pay for it.

We didn't even know who or what to ask of a TV station. Finally folks at the station told us that if we could tape the spot during the first commercial break in the late movie (20 minutes) we would not have to pay for production.

We developed a stupid idea with a birthday cake. When the voiceover blows out the candle the spot ends. Brilliant. At least we knew that it could be done within the 20-minute limit.

The day before we were scheduled to tape the spot, Dick Lewis called us with great news. He got Camilo Pascual, the All-Star 25-game-winning Cuban pitcher for the Minnesota Twins, to do the spot. In exchange Lewis gave him a car to use for the summer. Camilo was a very big deal.

I told Dick Lewis this would probably result in production charges. Again he said, "Get the stations to pay."

I asked Camilo to come early so we could rehearse. He was late. His first reading alarmed me. "Ah low, mi name Camilo Pascual here for sow tau cry sir pre mo." Hold it, Mr. Pascual. It's Southtown Chrysler Plymouth. "Ok. Sow tau cry sir pre mo."

We were running out of time. "Mr. Pascual, no matter what, don't stop reading the rolling script on the camera. Go all the way through and then blow out the candle at the end."

"Ah low, mi name Camilo Pascual here for sow tau cry sir pre mo, with good deal and rebates on cry sirs, pre mo, barracoo and wailant."

At the end he blew at the candle but missed. He looked up at the camera with the dumbest look on his face and we were out of time. What do we do now? Do we run the commercial later in the movie or do we have to buy the time and dead space ourselves? We took the risk of running Camilo.

We got a lot of phone calls the next day asking us how we got Camilo to be so funny. Many thought it was very creative.

From that point on Jack and I thought being a creative agency (instead of a brochure and logo agency) was in our future.

2850 Metro Drive

4120 Excelsior Boulevard

4069 Vernon Avenue

WORKSPACE

Out With Formality

ONE OF THE BENEFITS OF BEING THE BOSS (along with minority partners) was that I could decide where our offices would be located and what they would be like. I once read that most corporate offices were usually close to the CEO's home. That was true in my case, with one exception.

Jack Carmichael and I started Carmichael Lynch in a small two-bedroom house at 4069 Vernon Avenue in St. Louis Park. It was near Highway 100 and Excelsior Boulevard. I lived two miles away near Lake Harriet. (I have always lived as close to the city lakes as I could afford.)

After a couple years Jack and I expanded our offices to a colonial fourplex on Excelsior Boulevard. At first we occupied a lower and upper unit and then took over the whole building. It was a handsome building and a great step up from our humble Cape Cod. We put a basketball hoop over the double garage doors in the back for recreation. The place had four bathrooms we used for storage. We outgrew

Current location:
Wyman-Partridge Building,
110 North 5th Street

The Charles Pillsbury mansion, 100 22nd Street

The Alfred Pillsbury mansion, 116 22nd Street

800 Hennepin Avenue

this space once we had 30 employees and had to consider another move.

Much of our work was in the suburbs and near the airport. We became the first tenants at the new Metro Office Park in Bloomington. We leased the top floor with a huge patio on all sides. Every outside office had sliding glass doors onto the patio. We could see part of the old Twins stadium field.

We made that space into a fun place–roller skating, parties on the patio and outdoor meetings when the wind was calm. I bought a Macaw and trained it to speak when the elevator bell sounded. Squawk as the door opened, "Saw your ad," and squawk as the door closed, "Pay the bill." The bird was unique. One day someone scared it while it was perched on a small tree trunk on the patio. It jumped off and fell eight stories. Although its wings were clipped, the bird managed to swoop up just before it hit the ground and flew to a large oak tree in front of the Control Data office entrance. I called the fire department to retrieve the bird. They said cats were not supposed to be up in trees but birds belonged there. I then called the trainer who sold us the bird.

He tried to reintroduce the bird to my office. The poor thing was so antsy it would do nothing but sit on the back of a cane rocker and eat the webbing. Goodbye bird.

As we signed a five-year lease on the office space we realized rent was like a loan. We were responsible for repayment. Why not own our own office?

Even though the American Association of Advertising Agencies did not encourage agencies to own real estate, we began searching for something unique. We spent a lot of time looking at abandoned churches. One of our favorites was what is now the Russian Museum in south Minneapolis.

Our dreams were fulfilled when we found the Charles Pillsbury mansion near the Minneapolis Institute of Arts. The Institute was the seller and would take a contract for deed. It was an amazing historic house–103 stained glass window inserts and a fireplace that withstood the great fire of London in 1606. Another large carved wooden fireplace in the living room was equally old and unique because wooden fireplaces usually burned up. We were able to get both working again. We did a lot of remodeling while we kept the house on the Historic Registry. My partner Lou Bacig rode herd on the construction project and did a great job while having fun. Lou has always liked construction.

The mansion was quite a sensation. It garnered a huge spread in *Communication Arts. Fortune* magazine named it one of the five most interesting offices in America and ran a full-page photo of me sitting in the library. Boy, were my parents impressed.

It was a fabulous but drafty environment. That started a tradition. Each employee received a letter sweater with hash marks on a sleeve to mark the length of his or her employ. We were able to buy the Alfred Pillsbury mansion next door as we outgrew the Charles mansion. It was interesting but not as special as Charles. It did, however, have a secret bookcase that led to a stairway down to a vault. The Pillsbury family kept their famous jade collection there until they gifted it to the Institute. I had to have my office in the vault. How cool. I lasted two days. It was like being buried.

As the agency grew, we purchased two more mansions in the surrounding quadrangle but finally outgrew them all. Running between buildings and up and down many flights of stairs became very inefficient.

We again had to move and decided to move downtown. The employees were not enthusiastic about the move.

Terry came up with a great idea to soften their sadness about leaving. A funeral. A rite of passage. We dug a grave on the front lawn and each employee walked by and dropped his or her office keys into the grave. Then we paraded around the block led by a New Orleans funeral band, umbrellas and all.

The big leap. We purchased and rehabbed an eight-story, 100,000 sq. ft. building at the corner of Eighth and Hennepin. The area was a war zone. It was the city's drug and drunk center. Everything was boarded up and dirty. Many employees voiced concerns about their personal safety.

We did a creative rehab on the building and got press for its uniqueness. Everyone had a window (the interior offices were given a small glass block) and had the same 10'x 12' office with identical furniture. The décor of the 40 conference rooms was unique. A cow room for agriculture accounts, a Harley Davidson room, a baby room, a mansion room (with carpet and furniture from the Charles mansion), an urban graffiti room with corrugated steel walls that were spray painted, a fishing room...and on and on. They were fun. The creative department hung refrigerator doors on the walls and staff would tape their most recent work on the doors–just like you did when you brought your artwork home for mom to put on the frig.

We created a great work environment for 300 people. Carmichael Lynch also became a major force in the restoration of Hennepin Avenue.

Lou and I bought the building across the street, 730 Hennepin Avenue, for future expansion. For 15 years it was a great office and even greater investment for Lou and me.

When I retired from the agency the new management wanted to start a new chapter and move into new space. It saddened me but I understood. They wanted me to office in their new warehouse building. I thought it best to decline. I have never been back inside 800 Hennepin Avenue but have happy memories of our time there as well as at the mansions.

I often wondered how people could work in a drab, sterile office environment.

The agriculture accounts meeting room, The cow room, was one of 40 themed meeting spaces.

Annual summer picnic egg toss.

A client product parade to the new downtown office.

MANUFACTURING FUN

A Simple Plan For Retention

I REFERRED TO CARMICHAEL LYNCH as the "factory" when I was with financial friends. With 250 billable employees and a capacity to bill 1800 hours per year, I calculated that the factory had an inventory of 450,000 hours at $110 per hour which came to $49,000,000 of potential income each year. My job was to keep the factory busy and make sure the group and division leaders were creating a wake of activity for their staff rather than billing themselves out at $300 per hour. With leveraging you could bill entry-level employees at $110 per hour while paying them $20-$70 per hour. Using the 50-30-20 formula (50% salary, 30% non-salary and benefits, and 20% profit) you could easily see why Carmichael Lynch was the second most profitable (as a percentage of gross income) agency in the 4A's nationally.

The name of the game was to attract talented people and pay them well while billing clients at a premium rate. The work had to be of premium quality to keep a client. To keep employees we had to create an

No Stars softball team.

Leading the O'Gong Show.

The annual pet parade.

Rain gutter minnow races.

agency they were proud of and one that was a lot of fun to work for. The work was so demanding and the stress so high that engineering fun into the workday was a priority.

My job description was:

GET PEOPLE, KEEP PEOPLE, GET CLIENTS, KEEP CLIENTS

A succinct eight-word job description that only used four different words.

In 1990 we moved our offices from four mansions in south Minneapolis to an eight-story building downtown. We celebrated big with a symbolic departure from our old offices in the Pillsbury mansions to the new building downtown on 8th and Hennepin. We had a parade with products representing every Carmichael Lynch client. A marching band was in the lead and every employee participated.

The agency's attitude and physical environment were very loose and informal. No pretensions, no expensive décor, lots of open offices and 40 different themed conference rooms.

Christmas was a busy time and full of events. We paid bonuses on the last workday before Christmas. Every year we also gave each employee an unusual gift and closed the agency between Christmas and New Year's.

The best gift ever was from the secret Santa. A group of six people had the task of buying a gift for employees in their department based on a formula of $5 per month for the number of months they had been employed. (Employed for 12 months = $60, 24 months = $120, and so on.) Some people received baby carriages, airline tickets, a home bar, even a total golf outfit including sized clubs, shoes and clothing. When people first came to work at Carmichael Lynch they filled out a questionnaire asking such things as shoe size, favorite foods, etc. Later they marveled at how their boss knew exactly the right size. Of course the newest employee got a stupid gift.

The company Christmas party was a family event and with the move downtown, agency employees and family members became characters in the Holidazzle parade on the Nicollet Mall downtown. It was always a hit. The parade was followed by a family dinner back at the office.

March brought the O'Gong show which pressured each new employee to be in a talent show. I would begin the show by singing the *Vatican Rag* while dressed as St. Patrick. The O'Gong show today has a slightly different approach but remains an institution.

The month of May brought the season fishing opener and minnow races followed by a fish fry in the parking lot behind our office. Rain gutters were sealed at each end. Start and finish lines were drawn in before they were filled with water. Departments raced their special minnows against each other. There were pet and kid contests with prizes all relating to the sport of fishing. (Thank you, Rapala, for the prizes.)

The No Stars softball team was a hit every year. We weren't always winning but we were always winners.

July was time for the summer picnic. Lots of contests, beer, a skit performed by interns and good music. Sometimes the picnic was held in the parking lot and other times at a fun location around the city.

August was the dog parade. Employees brought their pets and kids to work on a Friday morning and at 11 a.m. everyone paraded down

Hennepin Avenue, blocking traffic. I was always the pooper-scooper. The event was often mentioned on the evening news.

October was usually a Halloween Party.

Summer hours plus the Christmas holiday break were the two most appreciated perks. Honoring birthdays, awarding excellence, celebrating awards, Friday soup days, blowing the bugle when a new account was landed and a monthly pizza lunch for new employees with the managing partners were all part of a concentrated effort to make Carmichael Lynch the most fun place to work even though you might make more money elsewhere.

Despite the enticing environment over a thousand people left Carmichael Lynch for various reasons over time. Retiring, fired, spousal transfer or lured away by a competitor. I took every departure (when a competitor got them) as a personal loss. I never minded when someone left to start his or her own business. At least 20 agencies in town grew out of Carmichael Lynch.

The greatest perk ever was the ESOP, the Employee Stock Option Plan. My partner Lou and I sold quite a bit of our stock to the ESOP at a low rate. That stock was then redistributed to employees, all employees, based on a percentage of their income. When people got their statements in the first few years they viewed the stock as funny money. Each year an appraisal of the agency's net worth was conducted. The stock became more valuable over time. The hook was you could not sell your stock for five years and when you left the agency the dollars accrued would be paid out over a period of years. It was a great plan and some of our higher paid employees saw some serious money accruing.

Lou and I were troubled that many employees were using the stock as their retirement plan. If the agency got into financial trouble they could be wiped out. That was one of the driving forces that made us consider selling to a public international holding company.

We sold to IPG in 1999. Many of our key players cashed out, some with as much as $900,000. We didn't expect so many to leave at the same time and it caused us no end of grief. The five-year moratorium on selling stock caused an artificial backup in resignations. But we survived.

We sold to IPG with a five-year autonomy clause. If we made our numbers (easy for us) I didn't have to return a phone call from New York. And I didn't. When the five years were up, I retired with the unique record of never having had a boss, other than Sgt. Hutchins, US Army.

JOHN MARKS

I Can't Hear You

John was a brilliant copywriter. He was well trained at the University of Iowa and later at a good agency with one big account. John wrote great stuff for the account and when he applied at Carmichael Lynch we hired him instantly.

John had trouble working with an art director, any art director. I thought pairing him with Jim Lotter, one of the top five in the Twin Cities, would help him come to his senses.

Jim tried but was constantly frustrated with John who did not accept any input from him. John also had trouble with the creative director, his boss. Jim insisted the boss become involved with John's unwillingness to listen to criticism. The creative director started closely monitoring his work and noticed that whenever he suggested a change John would not only resist but continue on the same path.

Things finally came to a head when Jim said he would no longer work with John. Nor would any of the other art directors. John's reputation had become widespread. The creative director consulted me about terminating John and I sadly agreed. He was such a great writer with a charming personality. Everyone loved John unless you had to work with him. It also turned out the clients John worked with didn't like his uncompromising attitude either. So John had to go.

His boss took him into his office and told him he was done and that we would give him a reasonable severance. John objected. He claimed we didn't realize what a mistake we were making and left saying that we would change our minds. The next day John showed up for work. The creative director again told him he was done. John again said that we would see the error of our ways and want him back. He wasn't going to leave.

The creative director came to me and described the situation. I was amazed at the lack of closure and told him we needed to meet with John together. I told John how upset we were that he had not left the agency and would shorten his severance if he didn't. John told me he knew I didn't have full command of the details and if I did I would not let him go.

The next day John showed up for work. I realized something very unusual was going on and called our industrial psychologist, Brad Swanson. Brad recommended we set up an appointment for John to see him. Brad had two meetings with John on two consecutive days and then called me to report. Brad said I was to come to his office and go through the process of firing John once again. It was weird but I did it. Brad wanted John to repeat every word I said to him. He did and started to understand the gravity of the meeting. John did not show up for work the next day.

Brad explained what was troubling John. He had polio as a kid and was told he would never walk again. I was amazed. John was a superb athlete and competitive bicyclist. Grade school became humiliating. Kids said he should be the base in baseball. John's dad was committed to proving the diagnosis wrong and worked with John every day to improve his leg muscles. For two years John went through a daily physical regimen as well as a mental one. His father taught him to ignore the doctors who said he wasn't going to walk again. Instead he should believe in himself and hard work. He would be playing ball in no time.

John did walk. He did play ball. And he was taught not to abide by bad news but to believe in himself. John was unable to hear criticism from his wife, kids, clients, partners and his boss. He had a psychological block that Brad Swanson helped him conquer.

John is now a freelance writer living in California. He has remarried and drops by on occasion to thank me for getting him to Brad Swanson. He makes me smile.

A TREMOR IN THE BLOOD

Fear, Not Truth

"You can tell a man is guilty by a tremor in the blood," said Daniel Defoe. *A Tremor in the Blood* is also the title of Dr. David Lykken's book about the lie detector and its reliability.

David was my next-door neighbor at 4600 Emerson Avenue in South Minneapolis and a well-known University of Minnesota psychology professor. David was also a consultant to the CIA on lie detection systems and uses.

Walter Goins was a new employee in the Carmichael Lynch film division in 1970 and a friend. He was going through a divorce and stayed at my house for a few months. Walter was a type A striver and master of many skills. He was a weekend disc jockey on a rock station and a licensed commercial pilot with twin-engine credentials. He joined our film group to learn about making movies. He was 24 at the time. Walter was also Black.

While living with me he got to know my neighbor David Lykken and was fascinated by his various studies and papers on identical twins.

The Carmichael Lynch film group needed to borrow a special high-speed, cold weather camera owned by our client, Arctic Cat, to shoot a product film about their new line of snowmobiles. Arctic's in-house photo group was disappointed. They had hoped the assignment would be given to them. The camera was expensive, more than $10,000, and kept in a lockbox at our office.

Somehow the camera turned up missing. The client advised us, in the case of theft, company policy was to hire a lie detection company to interview and test all the people who had access to the lockbox. Six people including Walter were tested. Everyone went downtown for the test and were quite giddy about the event. It seemed like a fun outing.

Of all people, Walter failed the test. Everyone had great fun kidding Walter and doctored a photo showing him behind bars. Walter was asked to retake the test.

He did, and once again failed. Everyone still took it lightly and kept teasing Walter, the "convict."

The Forsythe detective service felt that Walter may have taken the camera. Suspicion grew when they found out that Walter's former wife had just arrived in town with a trailer load of Mexican pottery for her new gift shop. Walter was disturbed and talked to his mother and father. She was on the faculty of the U of M law school and he was a doctor at the VA Hospital.

He retook the test under the supervision of his lawyer and once again failed. Forsythe reported to Arctic Enterprises that beyond all shadow of a doubt Walter stole the camera. Everyone was stunned.

His boss and workmates knew this was not possible and did some investigative work themselves. The camera had been pawned in Chicago by a Minnesota man. It turned out that man was the internal filmmaker at Arctic. The "team" apparently roughed up the culprit and got him to confess.

Thankfully I didn't have to ask Walter if he took the camera. I was a day away from giving Walter the bad news that he was fired and would be arrested.

David Lykken was fascinated by the case and wrote a magazine story for the *Saturday Evening Post* and later a book... *A Tremor in the Blood.*

Walter's case was a prominent part of the book's hypothesis asserting the lie detector measures fear not guilt.

David also noted that a Black man would be fearful, guilty or innocent. An overachieving Black man would be the most fearful because of his ambitions and goals.

David and I testified before the Minnesota Senate Judiciary Committee and later before the Senate Judiciary Committee in Washington, DC. David wanted the lie detector banned as evidence because of its lack of reliability. In 1988 the US Senate passed the Employee Polygraph Protection Act. David did note a lie detector could help trap a suspect when police had information only a criminal would know.

I heard years later that Walter acquired a low power license to operate a TV station in the Washington, DC area.

His success in later years could have been ruined by "the tremor in his blood".

THE GREAT SIGN THEFT

Back In The Slammer

LOU BACIG AND I, AS PARTNERS in 730 Hennepin Avenue (an office building across 8th Street from the Carmichael Lynch office), were close to considering a Texas closing on the building. (In a Texas closing you give the buyer some cash to take the property off your hands.) We had lost over a million dollars on it due to depressed downtown real estate prices. The building was mostly vacant and there were no likely prospects for the large space. That's until we got a call from Metropolitan State University. They were looking at space for a downtown campus.

Zowie! Lou and I agreed I would be the point person to spend whatever time and money was necessary to get them to the dotted line. We knew the rent for a state university space would not be profitable but it could stop the money hemorrhage.

Dan Kirk, an administrator at Metro State, said the faculty objected to moving to crime-ridden Hennepin Avenue. I knew their perception of crime on Hennepin was much higher than the reality. I had already asked the Minneapolis Community Development Agency (MCDA) and the Minneapolis Police Department for a microanalysis of crime on Hennepin.

I presented these findings to a ten-person search committee and they were impressed with the difference between perception and reality. In addition to allaying their fears, we sweetened the rental rate and time period and even guaranteed $50,000 in agency pro bono work for the University. They agreed to sign a five-year lease if, and only if, the full faculty voted to move to Hennepin Avenue. They scheduled a tour for a Saturday morning. Forty faculty members who opposed the move were going to tour and vote by noon. A make or break vote for Lou and me.

I asked the police department to chase off the usual derelicts and pan handlers, in fact anyone who looked strange. I got the city to sweep the streets early on Saturday morning and even replace the bent and sprayed trash cans with new ones.

The Skyway Lounge across the street had a sign in front of the door which blatently advertised *Dancing Nudes from Noon til Midnight.* The MCDA helped me get in contact with the owner (not easily done as he prefers to remain anonymous). I arranged to meet him at noon on Friday the day before the faculty tour.

I walked in the front door and was surprised by how small the place was. I was depressed by the look on the woman's face who was standing on the bar, nude, chastising a blearly old man who was waving money at her. The owner came out of the back room and gruffly asked me what I wanted. When I explained what was happening the next day and asked him to remove the sign for only a few hours he said only one thing before returning to his back room, "Fuck you."

Summarily dismissed, I left the bar and ran into Carmichael Lynch account supervisor Joe Sullivan and five or six of our McDonald's clients as they were going down the street for lunch. I don't think they believed my explanation why I was in a nudie bar at noon.

That afternoon I told Richard Buford of my dilemma and my plan to steal the sign. Richard, a thin, elegant Black man of about 50 was the agency's all around handyman and driver. Richard and I liked each other. Richard offered to help me steal the sign.

I told him not to worry about the police catching us because I forwarned them of my plan.

At about 4 a.m. we drove down Hennepin Avenue, with Richard behind the wheel of my 1990 Mazda pickup, and stopped at the curb in front of the Skyway Lounge. I jumped out of the truck and with some effort clipped the chain with a bolt cutter, threw the sign (which was heavier than I thought) into the rear end of the truck and got back into the cab.

As he drove off Richard said he couldn't believe he could go back into the slammer for stealing a nudie sign with his boss at 4 a.m. It was only then I realized Richard had a few secrets when he came from Kansas City.

The faculty came. They voted. They signed on the dotted line. They stayed for 15 years at market rate.

Later that afternoon we deposited the sign where we found it. I was sorry I didn't return the cut chain but somehow it got lost in the process.

Richard died a year later from emphysema. Shortly before he died he was at our cabin painting the deck of our pontoon. It was an activity he could handle because he could lay down and not exert himself too much. Richard knew he was dying as he lay there painting. We talked about it. And together we laughed one more time about the Great Sign Theft.

Minneapolis Tribune, *February 25, 1972.*

Robert T Smith

Lee Lynch has long hair, almost to his shoulders. He also is president of his own advertising and public relations firm — Carmichael-Lynch, Inc., of Bloomington.

Lynch, 35, is threatening to fire one of his employees because he has short hair. A put-on? It well could be, but Lynch is deadpanning it.

Lynch

Bacig

He says it's his retaliation for recent discrimination against long hair, including the firing of a long-haired Vietnam war veteran by Coon Rapids and the long hair squabble at Montgomery (Minn.) High School.

The victim in the Lynch case is Lou Bacig, 35, an account executive for the firm. Either he lets his short hair grow long or out he goes, says Lynch.

FEB 25 1972 T

"Do you know you can actually see his ears," said Lynch. "It's disgusting." According to Lynch and Bacig the Thursday morning session went like this:

LYNCH: "Sit down, Lou. You know, your work here has been excellent. You're one of our best. But you've got to do something about your hair."

BACIG: "But I have a right to have short hair."

LYNCH: "And I have a right to have my own grooming code in my own business."

BACIG: "My hair is no shorter than those three secretaries out there with the pixie cuts. Their ears show."

LYNCH: "But you're a guy, Lou. A girl can get away with short hair. But you're ruining the image of this firm. I've had several complaints from our customers. Look at it this way, Lou: Lincoln and Ben Franklin and Jesus, they all had long hair."

Bacig pointed out that President Nixon and J. Edgar Hoover and Art Linkletter all have short hair. "That proves my point," said Lynch.

BACIG: "I'm going to take my case to the Minnesota Department of Human Rights. I'll charge you with sex discrimination — allowing girls but not guys to have short hair."

LYNCH: "Go ahead. They've got so many cases of long-hair discrimination that it'll be years before they get to you."

LONG HAIRS ONLY

Peace Brother

THE VIETNAM WAR SPLIT AMERICA in many ways. "America, Love it or Leave it," or "Peace Now." There seemed to be no middle ground. If you were young, educated and had long hair you were most likely a subversive. If you were rural and older you were a patriot.

Business leaders throughout the country were behind the war. Communism had to be stopped from spreading throughout Asia and then on to the rest of the world. The domino theory prevailed. Some businesses adopted a dress code that did not permit long hair for men. No ponytails, beards or peace symbols.

One local company went so far as to fire an employee with long hair. I couldn't believe it. I chose to wear my hair long even though it disturbed some of my more conservative clients and prospects.

To make a point, with tongue in cheek, I fired my partner, Lou Bacig, for having short hair. I then asked all employees at Carmichael Lynch to grow their hair.

Robert Smith

MAR 3 - 1972

One man suggested that Lee Lynch be doused with gasoline and burned to death. And his short-haired employee should do it and be given a medal for it.

Other letter writers and telephone callers had similar suggestions. And the anti-longhair issue rolls on.

To try to show how ridiculous the whole issue is, Lynch, 35, president of Carmichael-Lynch Advertising, Inc., threatened to fire a short-haired employee, Lou Bacig, 35, an account executive.

Lynch

Bacig

In my column about it, I indicated it was a spoof. But Lynch's home phone started ringing at about 7 a.m. the morning it appeared . . . "How dare you? . . ." "You're not a good American . . ." "You're obviously a pervert . . ." "You're obviously a dirty Commie . . ." "You're a pervert and a Commie."

After some 40 calls of that nature by noon, Lynch had his secretary cut them off. He called me and I told him to let them through. Not one of the callers would identify himself or herself. So, Lynch devised a little plan:

"I told them they had the advantage. They knew me but I didn't know them. But no names. Then I said: 'This conversation is being taped for possible use on the radio. Maybe you're neighbors will recognize your voice.' In almost every case, they hung up immediately."

The next day the mail — all anonymous — started to flow and still is. Aside from the guy who wanted Lynch burned in gasoline, there were several Corinthian Elevens. They're the ones who use Chapter XI of First Corinthians to state their case. One line of that is: "Does not nature itself teach you that for a man to wear long hair is degrading to him . . .?" The Corinthian Elevens use this to back their contention that Christ had short hair.

"I was surprised at the number of responses and the venom displayed," said Lynch. "And, also, that so many took it seriously. Actually, most of them got angrier when they learned it was a spoof." Apparently, after they got through cussing out Lynch, they called Bacig. He received comfort and cheers and five job offers.

One reader who got the spoof, spoofed Lynch back: "You are in the creativity business which is the worst kind because it makes its practitioners think they can force apple-pie Americans to eat chicken kiev."

Well, the truth is out. Bacig is safe. Unless, of course, the first column was straight and this one is a spoof. Write soon.

Minneapolis Tribune, *March 3, 1972.*

Journalist Robert T. Smith at the *Star Tribune* heard about this and wrote a story about the event. In all his years as a columnist, he had never received such passionate and heavy response to a story.

His first column appeared on February 25, 1972.

Meanwhile I was bombarded with hate mail and phone calls at both my office and my home. Those kinds of people usually harass you anonymously. They never sign their names.

Robert T. Smith then wrote another full story the following week on March 3, when he heard about the harassment and read some of the letters I had received.

Those were divisive years.

KENNY O

The Constant Cigar

CARMICHAEL LYNCH ACQUIRED AN AGENCY called The Partners which introduced me to a well-known ad man, Ken Oelschlager. A former Campbell Mithun creative director and head of the early Bozell Jacobs office in Minneapolis, Ken was winding down his career when he and two other guys formed The Partners.

Ken was full of life experiences, both helpful and diverting. I enjoyed his company. He also helped me save the Tony's Pizza account when we really needed it.

Ken had polio as a kid which left him with serious lingering problems. His throat was still partially paralyzed. He had to keep exercising it by sucking on something all the time. Partially to disguise what he was doing, Ken chose to suck on a cigar morning, noon, and night. He ate alone and only ate one meal a day...breakfast. It took him almost two hours to eat because he could only take a small bite, chew it slowly and then stroke his throat to facilitate swallowing. No problem drinking though. He liked his scotch.

His throat constriction caused him to have frequent bizarre spells.

I was with him one day early in our relationship before I knew about his problem.

While walking across the IDS court downtown, Ken stopped and told me not to worry. He handed me his glasses, put his hat and briefcase down on the floor, went prone and passed out. Passing out caused his muscles in his throat to relax, allowing him to breathe.

Quite a crowd gathered. I had to tell them nothing was wrong. When Ken came to, he got up, brushed himself off, put on his hat and glasses, picked up his briefcase and nodded to the assembled crowd.

It happened again while Ken and I were flying to Las Vegas. I then knew why he insisted on an aisle seat. The cabin attendants were concerned when Ken got up, gave me his glasses and laid face down in the aisle (his napkin beneath his face) and passed out for about two minutes. I tried to calm everyone down but they didn't believe me until he woke up.

I feared Ken was not going to revive on one of these occasions. He lived to the age of 76.

GREY, GRAY, GREY

A Colorless Dinner

JERRY STAHL WAS A SENIOR EXECUTIVE at Carmichael Lynch in the late 90s. A key guy to the agency. Fortunately for him but not for me, Jerry was offered the CEO spot at the Minneapolis office of Grey Advertising, an international NYC-based company. Its largest account was Northwest Airlines and needed someone like Jerry to manage it effectively.

I was happy for Jerry. We held a unique going away dinner for him to celebrate his success. A Grey event.

510 Groveland was a hot restaurant with a private dining room that happened to have been painted gray. I arranged for Jerry's going away dinner to be held there. I ordered gray tablecloths, dishes, and napkins and arranged for a gray floral centerpiece.

The chef at 510 got into the theme of the event. Guests had only two choices for cocktails: Grey Goose martinis or Grey Riesling wine. Dinner was Arctic grayling, potatoes with a gray sauce, sautéed zucchini with Grey Poupon mustard and a gray flan for dessert.

The best part of the evening was the attire and entertainment. Everyone came in gray suits, gray ties and powdered their hair gray. It was a sight to behold. The evening ended with everyone telling non-funny jokes. The worse the joke, the funnier it was.

Me and Jerry Stahl.

FINANCIAL ADVICE

He Doth Protest

My partner Lou Bacig and I decided to hire the CPA who did our audit as chief financial officer. He was with a big eight accounting firm. He immediately saved us over $20,000 a year by doing the audit himself. He said that every three or four years he would arrange for an outside audit.

When it was time to renew our office lease, I started to think we should buy rather than lease. A mortgage and a lease were both obligations. The American Association of Advertising Agencies (4A's) did not recommend purchasing. Don't be in the real estate business. It's too distracting.

Nevertheless, we found a unique opportunity in a large mansion in south Minneapolis owned by the Minneapolis Institute of Arts. The building was in a quadrangle of other old mansions that were already being used as offices. These other buildings represented possible expansion opportunities.

The mansion, built by Minnesota pioneer Charles S. Pillsbury, was on the National Register of Historic Places. Its interiors were gorgeous with oak paneling, working fireplaces and 105 stained glass paintings in leaded windows. We could house 100 employees in the mansion after converting the servant's quarters and basement into offices.

Our CFO was against the idea. He was adamant but his arguments were not persuasive. He felt sure we could not qualify for a mortgage. The night before we were to sign the purchase agreement, he called me at home to confess. The agency was in financial disaster. He knew there would be an audit if we applied for a mortgage and his deception would be discovered.

I had based a portion of his bonus on how successfully he invested our cash float. Big mistake on my part. He and our broker at Merrill Lynch agreed in writing to limit the agency's cash float risk to no more than $100,000. The complicated options plan they designed far exceeded this agreement and placed us way beyond our limit. Way beyond.

I felt like I had been punched in the gut. $1,000,000 was at risk and growing. He kept doubling down and losing on a complicated options swap scheme.

I immediately called our attorney. This was a disaster, especially when we could lose our largest client which prepaid giving us a large float. We could not lose that client. They were threatening to fire us unless we hired more people with experience in their business category. I knew we couldn't hire three or four credible people fast enough but an agency with that experience was for sale. They had only one major account and were anxious to do a deal–no more anxious than we were.

Our client was willing to give them a chance even though they were a bit long in the tooth. This gave us a year to climb out of the financial hole our CFO put us in. We were profitable, stable and could be acquired if bad went to worse.

Some of our friendly competitors called to tell me the group we were about to acquire was soon to lose their only client. I knew that but didn't dare tell them the real reason for the purchase. They thought I was naïve.

Meanwhile, we fired both our CFO and the broker. We had to keep our reasons secret. If a huge financial loss became known, our bank could force us to pay all purchases up-front in cash. We could not get either of their licenses revoked because the word would be out.

Neither of them would face any penalty for their deception.

The end could have been worse. We didn't need a mortgage because the Art Institute was willing to sell on a contract for deed and the now $2,000,000 loss rebounded a bit after six months. In the end we only lost $600,000. Still a blow, but survivable.

A year later the mansion appeared in *Fortune Magazine* as one of the five most unusual office spaces in the nation.

Featured in Fortune Magazine *my office had a working fireplace that survived the 1666 great fire of London.*

A MEMORABLE WEDDING

The Devil In Me

AL FADDEN WAS A MINOR COMPETITOR to Carmichael Lynch. I respected the waves his agency, Fadden as in Cat, was making. Al liked me, and like so many of my competitors, I found him to be a fun and interesting guy.

Al asked me to be in his second (or possibly third) wedding to the lovely Pam Diamond and her family. I mention family because Al and Pam planned to invite Pam's parents to co-own a home with them on Lake Calhoun.

They both wanted their wedding to be a spectacle and that's what they got. The wedding ceremony was performed at the base of a steep dual staircase in a condo common space near the Mississippi River.

I was dressed as the devil and another friend was dressed as an angel. We stood across from each other about 15 feet above the couple who were standing at the base of the staircase. My role was to keep reminding Al of the good old days of being a single swinger. "Come on Al," the devil called out, "you are not a one-woman man. Remember Wanda? There's poker tonight Al, and she won't let you go." The devil went on and on. Meanwhile, the angel kept reminding Al of all his sins and urging him to settle down with Pam. Back and forth we went. The assembled audience loved the drama. Of course, the devil lost the argument and they were hitched.

The marriage lasted about five years. I don't know how the house and parents deal worked out, but what the hell. Quite a wedding.

A PAIR OF SINGLES

Saga Of The Lying Hunter

Our client, Arctic Cat, decided to hold their autumn planning session in rural North Dakota rather than at their offices in Thief River Falls, Minnesota. The rural location happened to be near Dry Lake, home to thousands of geese en route to their winter home. The conference attendees were all duck and geese hunters, so they planned to end the conference on Friday and rise with the sun on Saturday to go goose hunting.

They knew that I was not a hunter (and my wife at the time hated hunting of any sort) but insisted I go along with them to witness the grand event when the flock ascends from the lake.

I gave into pressure and got up at 4 a.m. to hike to the lake and wait in the cold for the birds to take off. They gave me a shotgun and told me not to shoot into the flock, but to wait for the stragglers…more sporting they said. About twenty of us were lined up along the shore spaced about 50 feet apart. It was cold.

As dawn started to break, I could hear geese getting ready to depart. Thousands rose through the mist on the lake just as the sun came up. It was an amazing scene. Truly awesome.

When the gigantic wave crossed over us, I could see the stragglers in the distance. The hunters along the line started shouting "single at 11," "double at 2," "single at 12." They were telling their fellow hunters where to look for stray geese. I was down at the end of the group with nothing in sight, thank goodness. But then, coming from my left I could see two geese flying low.

I shouted, "a pair of singles." I shot and missed and my adventure was over. Except when I returned to Minneapolis.

Little did I know that one of the hunters was Ron Schara, the outdoor reporter for the *Minneapolis Star Tribune.* Ron phoned in his story in time to make the Sunday paper.

When I walked in the door at home my wife didn't seem very happy. In fact, she was madder than hell. After all, I told her we had to work on Saturday. Then I saw the front page of the paper's sports section lying on the kitchen table. A "pair of singles" was the large headline for a story about a novice hunter who got so excited he didn't say "a double at 3." He called it a "pair of singles." Later, he was single.

NEAL CHENEY

He's Got A Gun

NEAL CHENEY WAS AN EMPLOYEE in the Carmichael Lynch accounting department. Although he was trained as a CPA his life was always on edge. Drinking. And drinking. Rehab and rehab again.

Neal was smart but undependable. He needed friendship and he found it in Bev Lockhart, the Carmichael Lynch 'house mother' and human resource person. She tried to help Neal and keep him straight. I was always nice to Neal and went out of my way to talk to him. I was known to visit everyone in the agency, but Neal thought he was special, that we had a special connection.

One night in October of 1982, I got a call from Bev to come to Neal's apartment. He had locked himself in and said he was going to kill himself. Neither Bev nor I thought Neal had the determination to take his own life. He didn't seem to be the type. We thought he was asking for attention.

I met Bev at his basement one-room apartment. Neal would not answer the door and let us in. He finally started to talk to Bev and when he found out I was there he wanted to talk to me. He told me about his failures and said he had a gun and was going to do it right now. I stalled him thinking he didn't actually have a gun and kept trying to get him to open the door.

He finally said only I, no one else especially the police, could come in. I hesitated for just a moment. Bev said don't do it, he may really have a gun. I said he was going to shoot himself not me, or so I thought. I didn't think he had a gun. Neal was a small guy and I didn't think he could even fire one and so broke he couldn't buy one.

I went into the dark apartment, closed the door and talked to Neal in the dark. At my urging he finally turned on a light. It was a tiny room with only a table, a single bed and one chair. Neal was sitting on the bed with what looked to be a 45 revolver. A big gun. I sat in the chair as Neal picked up the gun and set it on his knee. He was crying.

Just for a moment, I thought he might shoot me.

I promised I would not turn him in to the police but said I was going to take him to treatment. He went into St. Mary's rehab center. He never came back to work.

Years later Neal called me and asked for his old job back. When I told him there was no position for him, he cried. He never called again.

The Pope was quite surprised when the nuns shed their habits.

THE O'GONG SHOW

Tacky, Tacky, Tacky

THE O'GONG SHOW STARTED at Carmichael Lynch with the move downtown. Green had become the agency's color scheme so it seemed only natural to celebrate St. Patrick's Day in an unusual way. Anyone who claimed Irish roots was invited to breakfast at the mansions – green eggs, green juice, green beer and green Bloody Mary's. With the move downtown, the breakfast didn't seem to be celebratory enough. Something needed to be added. A talent show was the answer and the O'Gong show began.

It was a tacky event in its early years. I wore a dreadful St. Patrick's costume and the few acts were generally lame. Gradually a few stars started to emerge. The event was held in the first-floor glee club area and could be seen easily by all employees, clients and best of all, the people looking in the window from the bus stop. It was a great place to hold a show and over the years both the costumes and acts improved. Pressure was put on all new employees to perform in some way and they usually complied. The show swung into high gear when several senior staffers got involved.

Annie Callanger performed one of the most memorable acts. Dressed in a pilot's outfit with a snoopy earflap cap she explained to everyone that she was going to step outside on the Hennepin Avenue sidewalk and catch a golf ball dropped from the eighth floor in her teeth. With an intense drum roll, the first two balls dropped, missed her and bounced out into the intersection. The third attempt brought the house down as she caught it and instantly ran into the lobby to take a bow. She won the prize for the best act of the day. At the end of the event she demonstrated how she did the trick. She had an accomplice hang out of the second-floor window and drop a marshmallow for her to easily catch in her teeth.

I always opened the O'Gong show dressed as St. Patrick singing the *Vatican Rag*, an old Tom Lehrer song. As time went on, I donned a Pope costume and was joined by a chorus line of nuns to assist me in a dance routine. At first, the nuns were some of the older women in the agency which made it a funny bit.

As the show grew in both size and renown we had to move to a larger venue. The First Avenue nightclub could accommodate everyone who wanted to attend. The production values went up for me as well as the other performers. My nun chorus line was always a surprise. One year a group of men dressed as nuns. Another year the Timberwolves cheerleaders performed.

Best of all, the last year I appeared in the show I hired professional dancers. They choreographed a whole routine. They dressed as nuns and as we sang the last verse, they removed their habits revealing their skimpy costumes as they surrounded the pope. When we practiced they wore baggy sweatsuits. Then the performance. I was stunned to see a great deal of skin. They were in particularly good shape.

Singing and dancing as the Pope seemed to satisfy my acting gene.

MINNESOTA FATS

Very Mad Men

My partner Lou and I were in desperate need of good management advice as the agency grew larger. The 4A's (American Association of Advertising Agencies) was a logical source for such advice but Carmichael Lynch didn't meet its net worth membership requirements. We didn't make much money in the early '70s and certainly didn't put any profits into net worth. We bonused out all profit to compensate for being underpaid.

In early spring of 1975 a representative of the 4A's, Tony Lewis, asked if he could visit us. He wanted to talk about membership. We were nervous because we knew he would want to see our balance sheet. He came but never asked about our financial strength. We told him we were profitable but didn't have any net worth. We were stunned when he said as long as we made money it didn't make any difference. Many agencies our size did the same thing. He then spent two hours talking about all the benefits of being a member. Needless to say, he could have saved his breath because we were already sold. The only thing left was to give him a check for membership and send our financial statement to the 4A's executive director, Harry Pasteur. Uh oh.

Two months later I met Harry. He called to say he had some concerns. We could be members but on probation. His concern was not our lack of net worth but our ownership of the office building, the Pillsbury mansion. He contended that it was unwise for agencies to own real estate. He believed it would distract us from our advertising mission causing us to spend too much time, money and energy in managing the real estate and not the agency.

That year we were quite profitable. We left a little on the bottom line and were taken off probation. I went to my first 4A's annual meeting at the Greenbriar resort in White Sulphur Springs, West Virginia. I was surprised by the old sleepy time elegance of this famous resort. I was even more surpised by how everyone knew each other, except me. Everyone had a spouse, except me. Harry Pasteur liked me and made sure I met the right people and sat at the right tables. That's when I met Dick and Rita Seclow who became good friends. Harry also encouraged me to attend the annual meeting every year. He urged me to work hard at building relationships with peers and to stay in touch with them during the year. He believed it would help us enormously in the long run. I thought he was doing a sell job for the Association but it turned out to be really good advice. I did make an impression that year.

There was always a golf tourney during the annual meeting. This year it was on Sam Snead's course at the Greenbriar. I was placed in a foursome with Dick Durrell, publisher of *People Magazine*, Patrick McGrath of Jordan Case & McGrath, a merger and acquisition guy from New York and me. I rented clubs and shoes and didn't have a handicap because I didn't belong to a golf club. I told them I would shoot 95 (I hoped I would) and they included me in a complicated bet. Everything went right from the first tee on. I had good bounces on bad shots, chipped in two shots, drained long putts and in one instance hit a ball into a creek only to have it hit a rock and bounce on to the green. The results–39 on the front nine and 45 on the back. For a total of 84 and $420 from my partners. They thought the boy from Minnesota had conned them. That night I won two glass Tiffany bowls for the low gross and the low Callaway. I took the stage and received the gifts from Bob Hope, the entertainer for the evening. Years later Dick Durrell came to Minneapolis and told this story at a large dinner sponsored by *People*. Only then did Lou and others believe me. I never played in the golf tourney again. I switched to tennis.

The following two years I took sister Karen and my daughter Kate to the meetings at the Greenbrier (it was held there three of every four years). Our creative reputation was rising. I got to know quite a few people. Karen and Kate were popular. I started winning the tennis tourney every year...more Tiffany gift certificates. And more important I started to glean valuable information from my newly found friends. Terry was an instant hit at her first meeting. We looked forward to the event every year.

Harry went to bat for me again by getting me named secretary/treasurer of the 4A's board, the highest slot a medium-sized agency could hold in the organization. Although the title was for show it did give me insight into how the "big" guys lived and thought. They weren't as smart as I expected. I surprised the crowd at the next annual meeting by singing the treasurer's report to the tune of Gilbert and Sullivan's *Modern Major General.* Allen Rosenshine, Omnicom's president, couldn't believe it. I was told it was the first time anyone listened to the financial report. Years later he became one of our prospective buyers.

In 1990 the Association established a new award, the A+ Award, to recognize agencies that could demonstrate creative consistency over ten different clients. It was one of the few years I was going to miss the annual meeting. Harry called and said you gotta come. Carmichael Lynch is the winner of the first A+ Award.

Lou and I couldn't believe it. We didn't until the three finalists were named at the big banquet. Even then, we could hardly believe we beat BBDO, New York and Leo Burnett, Chicago. But we did. We finished in second place in 1991 and won it again in 1992. Only then did Burch Drake, the new executive director of the Association, tell me that Carmichael Lynch had really won in 1991, but they felt the contest would die if a medium-sized agency won in the first two consecutive years, especially when the competition was designed for large agencies.

In 1995 I was asked to make a presentation at the annual meeting about Carmichael Lynch's unique culture. That was fun. But not as much as my presentation in Bermuda in the spring of 2000. My topic was "Cashing In and Cashing Out" I had fun with the audience of peers as I moved from one side of the room to the other and back again giving a phony reason for why we sold out (international connections) and then from the other side of the room the real reason (CASH). My presentation received the highest score at the annual meeting. A good one to go out on.

Over the years we went against the recommended policies and management practices of the group. We switched to fee for service and true agent when the industry was trying to hold onto the 15% commission system of compensation. We became an ESOP when it was considered a bad move. We continued to own our real estate until the ESOP came into being and then transferred the real estate into our own names.

Being members of the 4A's was invaluable as we built the agency and ultimately was part of the reason Carmichael Lynch snagged a premium price from IPG, a large international agency holding company.

Looking back we should not have sold. The international holding companies had little to offer. Most of our ample profits (we always earned 14% after-tax) now were going to New York.

Lou and I made the prudent decision to sell to protect our employees' ESOP retirement funds. We can both be proud we shared the wealth with all of our employees, making a few of them quite well off.

I no longer was essential to the success or failure of the agency. I had no responsibilities and could come and go as I pleased. My greatest value in those years was to play Solomon when the managing partners had disputes and to imbue the culture and history of the agency to new employees. The current managing partners made it very easy for me to let go of my "baby."

It took a bit longer to get out than I planned. After two attempts the succession plan worked. The 800 Hennepin Avenue building was excluded when we sold the agency stock. Lou and I retained ownership of it. We charged the agency rent at New York rates. After two years IPG lawyers told us the rent was too high. I said, "Duh."

Carmichael Lynch will celebrate its 60th anniversary in 2022.

CIVIC ACTIONS

Trying To Change The System

AMERICA'S WORST POLITICAL ADS

Every four years during several presidential elections I organized an event called the Academy Awards of Bad Political Ads. It became a popular fundraiser for the non-profit Growth and Justice, a progressive think tank headquartered in Minnesota. The archives of the University of Oklahoma journalism department were a rich source of material. There were award categories, celebrity presenters and a grand prize for the worst Democratic and Republican commercials.

The Willie Award was named after the infamous Willie Horton ad that helped elect George H. W. Bush as president. The Daisy Award was named after a nuclear scare commercial for Lyndon Johnson running against Barry Goldwater. Many in the political world in Minnesota attended the event. I had hoped they would get the message and refrain from stooping to the low national norm. Unfortunately, Minnesota candidates still often hired the same slime masters out of DC to run ads which insulted our intelligence and good taste.

The event became popular enough to sell out the 1,000 seat Pantages Theatre in downtown Minneapolis. Generally three or four finalists qualified in each of the seven categories.

THE CITIZEN'S CAMPAIGN ADVERTISING CODE

Political advertising was hitting new lows with each new election cycle. I believed that negative advertising was suppressing voter turnout and making us all incredibly cynical.

In response to these concerns, I developed a Code of Conduct for candidates which permitted comparative advertising provided the candidate appeared on screen and delivered half of the commercial. I thought that the "meanness" would be modified if the candidate had to say the words him or herself.

The code was launched just before the explosion in dark money and special interest PAC advertising.

I formed a non-profit with a well-known and politically balanced board:

- KEN DAYTON, *Democrat and large campaign contributor*
- ED SPENCER, *Republican and* CEO *of Honeywell*
- *Two former chairmen of both parties*
- *Two retired congressmen*
- *Two retired judges*

I hired two staff to help me get candidates to sign our Code of Conduct. We had some good press exposure. I made several speeches to groups from the League of Women Voters to the Better Business Bureau. Surprisingly a big obstacle was the current chairmen of each party.

When Senator Paul Wellstone found out the DFL chair was dragging his feet he went ballistic. Wellstone was a big supporter of the idea. The Republican chair urged his candidates not to sign. Taking away negative, misleading advertising would deprive the candidate of an important tool. Despite his objections some Republican and almost all Democratic candidates signed on.

Although I intended the code to be applied only to federal races and state constitutional officers, several state house and senate members wanted to sign on as well. Smaller state races use direct mail as their primary media (in addition to lawn signs) and that's where the dirty work went. The two retired judges on the board agreed to rule on fairness in direct mail.

The idea failed. Dark money and special interest PAC's ran commercials, supposedly not tied into campaigns, using mean, misleading and untruthful advertising. We could not stop them. Candidates let them do the dirty work.

My code was finished. Political advertising is free speech and protected by the Constitution and could not be stopped. As time went on it got worse with each election cycle. The 2018 midterms witnessed a new low.

A MORE SUCCESSFUL CAMPAIGN

Since the beginning of time politicians have railed against high taxes. Minnesota, a high tax state (usually in the top ten high tax states), did not seem to be a fertile place to advocate for higher taxes but an ad hoc committee of successful businesspeople did just that. The four leaders of the cause were Jim Pohlad of the Pohlad family, Joel Kramer, former publisher of the *Minneapolis Star Tribune*, Dick McFarland, founder of a large brokerage business, and me. We argued a 2% surtax on incomes above $150,000 on individuals and $250,000 on married couples would maintain the state's commitment to its renowned high quality of life while also keeping it fiscally sound. Minnesota is one of the few states in the nation with top bond ratings.

I made many calls to enlist those who believed that the 2% increase was fair. Our efforts succeeded. The legislature passed the 2% increase in 2013.

Not everyone was happy with me. Many people suggested I send a personal check to the state capital if I loved paying more taxes so much. My dear Republican sister said I embarrassed her.

Oh well, you can't win them all.

Jack posed for his own funeral.

Jack and me at Carmichael Lynch's 50th Anniversary.

JACK, ALWAYS CREATIVE

An Unusual Memorial Service

I MET JACK CARMICHAEL IN 1957 while I was a copy boy and tour guide at the *Minneapolis Star and Tribune.* Jack and I often played chess in the projection room. He was a production artist and a very gentle guy.

Jack was one of the first people I called when I got out of the Army in 1962. He had left the *Star Tribune* and was a freelance artist working out of his home. When I went to see him, he was upset because the copywriter who was to work on a brochure was sick and Jack was under the gun.

I looked at the assignment and decided I could do it. I worked all night and successfully presented the work the next morning. The client gave me another assignment and a check for the first job. Since I needed immediate income, I decided to miss an interview at General Mills and take a job with Jack.

I never did go to any of the other interviews I had scheduled. Instead I started selling "log ohs" and brochures for Jack until someone told me it was pronounced "low go". That was the beginning of Carmichael Lynch.

In 1969 the agency got larger and Jack's drinking problems greater. I knew Jack had to leave the agency. It was only seven years after we started. Jack was ready to go. He hated the fact that Carmichael Lynch was getting bigger and more corporate even though we had only 20-30 people on staff at the time.

Jack became a full-time professional game inventor and did fairly well until electronic games came along. He was strictly a board game inventor. He later moved to Las Vegas and worked as a freelance creative.

Jack retired from advertising but kept creating big ideas. He started a program called Drivers Edge. He had witnessed a noon hour car crash that killed six high school girls in Vegas and thought it would be a good idea to develop a driver's training program for teens, focusing on high-speed driving. Jack believed teens thought they were great drivers and could handle high speeds under all conditions. He found local sponsors and set up a driving course in a large parking lot. Kids drove through pylons, turned on gravel and experienced oil slicks all at high speed. The teens and sponsors were surprised. The program went national. Jack's daughter became a full-time coordinator for the program.

I was proud of him. As the program grew Jack was no longer needed. He was never the administrator the program required.

I visited Jack in 2010 to see how he was doing. He was full of religion. He wrote three books, all fiction with a Christian theme, and developed some kid's books and games. He was back creating.

The next time I saw Jack was at the 50th anniversary of Carmichael Lynch. He was happy to be there and loved the attention. I found out the next day that Jack and his wife JJ had just walked away from their home in Las Vegas and moved into a rental. Unfortunately Jack had taken out several second mortgages to help his kids and was nailed by the implosion of housing prices in Las Vegas.

Jack died at 81. The funeral was in Las Vegas and the reception that followed was unique. Tables and chairs were set up in a very large room. One of Jack's games was placed on each table. Everyone at the reception took turns playing his games.

Love birds at ages 44 and 39.

COURTSHIP OF TERRY

A Slow Burn

I HAD PLANNED ANOTHER RIVER TRIP—climbing in Peru, a white water raft down the Andes, then proceeding on to the upper Amazon. But the trip was canceled. Since I had scheduled the time to be away I looked for something else to do. The Aspen Institute had a cancellation in its executive seminar program so I enrolled to study the great books with Mortimer Adler for two weeks.

When I arrived I realized most of the class would be re-reading the great books and I would be hitting them for the first time. Adler was not available so Norvel Morris, dean at the University of Chicago Law School, served as the moderator. The class was made up of oil execs, a drug exec, one Saudi prince, Angier Biddle Duke, a BCG consultant, a Coke executive...and me.

Terry Saario was one of two specialists whose job was to keep the facts straight. I wasn't interested in her during the seminar until the last day when she invited me to lunch. We all departed the next day. I didn't think much about her until four months later when Aspen sent photos of the class. Then I remembered how special she was. By then I was separated from my wife and decided to call Terry in Washington, DC.

She answered my call. I asked her to have dinner with me in DC. She said she couldn't because the moving van was there at that very moment, she was moving back to New York. I paused to think up an alternative. The phone seemed dead to Terry although she knew the line was still open. After opening with "Hello, I'm Lee Lynch and I'll be in Washington this weekend," I changed it to "Hello, I'm Lee Lynch and I'll be in New York this weekend." She fell for it and agreed to have dinner with me.

I asked her what show she would like to see. She tested me by saying she would like to go to *Evita* (which had recently opened on Broadway). I was in luck because Jimmy Stein who played Che in the show was from Minneapolis. I called my friend John Davidson and he arranged for Jimmy Stein's fifth-row center seats. Terry was impressed.

I asked her if I could see her the next night. She tested me again by asking for tickets to Lena Horne's new one-person show. I was stumped.

The next morning I went to the Broadway ticket office for Lena's performance. I was going to ask the ticket agent how to find a scalper. He was on the phone. I waited and as he put the receiver down he said, "You must be Irish. I just had a cancellation of two house seats." Front row center.

We arranged to go to dinner before the show. Leaving the restaurant we were met with a heavy downpour and long taxi lines. Only a Midwesterner would do something as gauche as hailing a hansom cab in the rain. We made the performance on time.

Lena shook her sweat on us. It was a great show. Terry thought the kid from Minneapolis was really connected in the Big Apple. The rest is history.

MESS'N WITH TERRY

Talk About Gullible

LEARNING ABOUT MINNESOTA

My wife Terry's first year in Minnesota was a learning experience. She was a transplanted New Yorker with a La-La background and little exposure to the Midwest. She had spent more time in France than her combined time in 12 Midwestern states. It became my job to help her understand us.

Her first visit to the cabin took us past many prosperous farms. She was quite curious about the tall domed cylinders we saw along the way… silos. "I'm surprised to see so many observatories," she noted.

I told her that the University of Minnesota had a very vibrant astronomy program. When we passed two silos built next to each other she wondered why. I told her more than one observatory was needed because of the perfect viewing conditions in that location and the demand of 56,000 curious students.

As we passed more and more, she seemed to doubt my word. I told her that other local colleges built their observatories to compete with the U of M. "There's Carleton's, St. Thomas's and St. Olaf's." She seemed to buy the explanation.

Then we passed a smaller silo. She caught me when I said it was built for kids because their eyes are weaker.

PUBERTY

Early on Terry asked me how I could stand the cold weather in Minnesota. I replied one's ability to adapt to extremes was triggered by where you lived when you went through puberty. I lived in Minnesota when I went through puberty. Terry lived in Southern California. The same force explained why she preferred hot weather. She accepted the explanation. The issue didn't come up again for a few months until Terry told some of her friends about the puberty theory. They wondered how she could be so gullible. Where did she get her PH.D.? Puberty theory? She was irate with me for mess'n with her.

ZUCCHINI

Her first vegetable garden at the cabin was quite a success, especially for a New York City gal. The zucchini she planted were prospering–getting bigger and bigger by the day. I told her they were remarkable. She started to give them special fertilizer and water. Before long they were larger than footballs.

I suggested she share them with friends since she had grown more than we could eat. She proudly picked them, washed them and even put a red ribbon around them. As she went to deliver the zucchini, I called ahead and told our friends to go crazy with compliments. She was so proud of her first crop. Little did she know that a large zucchini is woody and tasteless.

She was pissed at me when she found out I had fooled her. I agreed it was mean and I promised never to do it again. She never planted zucchini again.

POWER COUPLE

Without Real Power

IN THE MID-80S, THE LOCAL PRESS BEGAN TO WRITE about "power couples," married couples with high profile jobs. My wife Terry and I became the subject of such articles. The label suggests the couple has unusual access or power. Not so. These stories only encouraged people to solicit us more aggressively for contributions or donations.

Terry was president of the Northwest Area Foundation, which gave away jillions of dollars each year to certain focused projects. Everyone wanted a piece of that largess, a piece of the action. She was also chair of the SPCO board and led it through a major turnaround from annual deficits to a solvent world-class orchestra. Terry was mentioned often as a possible candidate for the US Senate. In her spare time, she was on three or four corporate boards.

Business Week magazine cited her as one of the top five foundation executives in America.

We were invited to everything and at times it got to be too much.

Together we were chairs or board members of many nonprofits such as the Minneapolis College of Art and Design. We held more than 100 fundraisers for local and national democratic candidates.

Meanwhile I was the co-founder and CEO of Carmichael Lynch, a major advertising agency with a large local profile in the Twin Cities and known to support many local causes. I was president of the regional American Association of Advertising Agencies and went on to become the secretary-treasurer of the board of the national organization. Carmichael Lynch was ranked one of the top 25 agencies in America, employing over 300 people and adding to the cachet that led the Twin Cities to become one of the top four agency cities in America. *Graphis*, an international design and advertising magazine, named Carmichael Lynch one of the top ten creative agencies in the world.

I co-founded and was the first chair of the Historic Theatre Group, which led the restoration of the State and Orpheum Theatres in downtown Minneapolis. HTG had both a for-profit component and a nonprofit arm. Both the restoration of the theaters and the method of financing the restorations became a big hit in the community. The city issued bonds for the restoration which were paid off by adding a $2 to $4 fee on every ticket sold. My partner Fred Krohn and I led the for-profit entity for 18 years while the nonprofit was spun off for entertainment tax purposes. Nonprofits like the Ordway, Orchestra Hall and the Guthrie were not required to pay the 10% tax on tickets. We had to become a nonprofit to be competitive. We maintained a for-profit status for speculation and other activities.

Both Terry and I believe in giving back, by being active in the community. Together in our 40 years of marriage we were on 30+ boards and special committees.

As a shareholder in the Carmichael Lynch employee stock option plan, brother Tommy said he was going to fire the CEO.

BROTHER TOMMY

Against All Odds

MY OLDER BROTHER TOMMY WAS BORN with cerebral palsy in 1929 at the depth of the depression. He was sent home from the hospital in a curled fetal position. Doctors were not optimistic Tommy would ever walk.

My father didn't accept this diagnosis. He organized friends in Belle Plaine to volunteer to take one-hour shifts for 16 hours a day to apply hot compresses on Tommy's muscles. This could only happen in a small town. Slowly it seemed to work. Tommy was able to move his limbs, then crawl, then walk with an awkward gait.

His early years were spent at the Michael Dowling School for Crippled Children in St. Paul. My father had to find a loving home in the cities where Tommy could stay when he wasn't in school. Tommy had a series of wonderful old dolls who took care of him over the years. Every Friday night Tommy would take a Greyhound bus to Belle Plaine for the weekend. He was such a regular that the driver violated company rules and dropped Tommy off in front of our house.

In his early teens Tommy was placed in the third-grade class at St. Peter and Paul's school. My school. I felt embarrassed about all the problems Tommy was causing. He simply could not read. My Dad's solution was to find a sheltered workshop where Tommy could work. Tommy was gregarious and loved to be in a group. Dad drove him to the workshop 40 miles each way every day.

Tommy remained in sheltered settings and rooming houses for almost thirty years. He became a valued member of the 250-person Carmichael Lynch workforce when we moved to a building with an elevator in downtown Minneapolis. Tommy met his boss, Frank Ramator, on his first day of work. Tommy was told I was not his boss and he had to work for Frank. Day one started under a dark cloud.

Frank gave Tommy an industrial broom and told him one of his responsibilities each day was to sweep the sidewalk around the office building.

Tommy was very social, very friendly. He loved talking to street people. He stood his broom against the wall of the office building as he talked to a group of homeless folks. When he turned around he realized his broom was missing. Someone had taken his broom.

He was frantic. He spent the day going from store to store downtown to see if he could find a similar broom for sale. He returned at 5 p.m. expecting Frank to fire him...after only one day.

Tommy soon became a beloved employee. Everyone liked him and was kind to him. He especially loved getting shares of stock through the Carmichael Lynch employee stock plan. He threatened to fire me.

Tommy spent weekends riding a metropolitan bus with his good friend and bus driver, Richard Buford. He could proudly negotiate the metropolitan bus schedules and get anywhere by bus, including meeting us at the gate at the airport.

Housing for Tommy was always a problem until Nancy Lahr came along. Nancy was a godsend. Mary Paulson, a senior executive at the agency, recommended Nancy to us. Nancy needed stability in her life, both financially and emotionally.

I rented a two-bedroom apartment at The Kenwood apartments, an assisted living facility, where both Tommy and Nancy could live together. We bought Nancy a car so they could be mobile. We treated her like family and she was. She took care of Tommy through 12 happy years.

Nancy's sudden illness and death broke Tommy's heart and spirit.

He moved into assisted care and died a year later from old age and the effects of cerebral palsy.

Tommy enriched all our lives.

October 17, 1926 – September 10, 2006

TOM LYNCH IN IRELAND

A Northern Cork Man

I TOOK MY DAD TO IRELAND IN THE LATE 70S. He frequently went to Canada to fish and traveled to Mexico several times but had never been east of St. Paul. Flying to his ancestral home was a big event for him and a great one for me.

He didn't want to stay in fancy places. He wanted to stay at bed and breakfasts and avoid the tourist hot spots. He wanted to get to meet some local people. More importantly, he wanted to see his family farm in County Cork. We worked with a search firm and were able to trace its location but had no idea what we would find.

I rented a car and we started to explore most of Ireland. Most of the B&B's were farms which suited Dad well. It was a simple life. The first week I was a bit bored. But soon I got into the simplicity of Irish life and the many pubs we frequented.

While on the highway driving to Galway, I noticed that Dad did not seem to understand some of the highway signs as they were a bit different from US signs. I thought it was a vision problem. I asked him when he last had his eyes examined. I was stunned by the response.

He could barely read. There I was, driving on narrow roads at 60 mph learning my father couldn't read.

It explained a lot of things about him and our family. Dad was kicked out of school in the 7th grade. Dumb kid. Couldn't read. He was told to learn a trade. He spent the next few years hunting and fishing almost every day and hanging out with men considerably older than he was. Finally, his brother Frank, aka "Shorty," asked Dad to join him in his barbershop.

They barbered for years until the great depression. Haircuts could be put off or done at home. Business was terrible. Dad saved a receipt from his worst day. Fifteen cents. Somehow I lost that receipt. He vowed then to get into another line of work as soon as possible.

"Everyone needs insurance," he always said. When he found out he could pass the insurance exam orally he had brother Frank read all the books to him. He passed the exam and started to sell life insurance to his customers in the barbershop while they were captive in the chair. "I always talked about life insurance when I had a razor near their throat." Business was slow but it was better than barbering.

Then came the big break. The State of Minnesota passed a law requiring mandatory automobile insurance. He had the only license in town. Farmers stood in line in front of the barbershop to get insurance. From that day on he put down the shears and razor and became "Thos. H. Lynch, Insurance Man."

There never were any books in the house when I was young. The radio was always on and we had the first TV in town. It all now made sense. Only my mother and his secretary, Erma Schlingman, knew he couldn't read.

We talked about this for hours in the car and again in the pubs. I was spellbound.

We also discussed homosexuality. Dad had concluded that one of every ten people was gay based on observing sheep. To prove his point, we spent a few hours watching hundreds of sheep grazing. His conclusion seemed valid. I talked him into walking out to the flock, getting down on his hands and knees and pretend he was eating grass. I had him wired for sound and heard him say on tape, "These sheep are looking pretty good to me. I think it's time to go home to your mother."

I never knew that my dad had an accent until we were in Killarney shopping for some gifts to bring home. While I was looking for a shirt, I heard the old man behind the counter greet my father and ask him where in northern Cork he was from? The old man was surprised when my dad told him he was from Belle Plaine, Minnesota. The old man replied that dad looked like a Cork man and sounded like a northern Cork man. I immediately grabbed my video camera and had them re-enact the dialogue. They were terrible actors but I got the story on tape.

In tracing the family history in Ireland I discovered everyone in the family not only married mates from Cork but from northern Cork.

Eventually, we found the farm that was supposed to be the Lynch original. It was beautiful but run down. High on a hill overlooking three lakes, it looked like a scene from a movie. In the front yard, in a wheelchair sat 94-year-old Patrick Lynch and his frail wife. Patrick was blind but quite a talker. My dad loved it. He asked about a woman in her 60s who was taking care of various household tasks. Turns out she left the convent to come home and take care of her parents. Dad noticed an old car up on blocks. They explained that they didn't have the $400 to fix it so it had been sitting there for quite some time.

My father was a prudent man. Ultra-frugal but he gave them the money to fix the car.

We left the Lynch farm happy campers.

A decade later, Cousin Eileen Effertz sent us a book on the Lynch family tree. It turns out the Lynch's were not lace-curtain Irish from County Cork but were from shanty County Meath. Apparently people from Meath had a northern Cork accent.

It seems everyone from Ireland comes from Cork not because they were raised there but because that's the point of debarkation to America.

"Where did you come from?" County Cork.

Tom and Ethel at their 65th anniversary party.

SURPRISING TOM AND ETHEL

We Surprised Ourselves

It's fun to surprise loved ones. We pulled off a big one for my mother and father's 65th wedding anniversary. We invited everyone in Belle Plaine to attend through a full-page ad in the *Herald* showing their wedding day photo and asking everyone to bring just one flower to the celebration. The *Herald* went along with the plan and removed that page from my parent's paper. They knew nothing about the event. It worked. They were genuinely surprised.

Our kids and grandkids were responsible for setting up a huge tent on their front lawn. Everyone had precise tasks and had to accomplish these while Dad and Mom were taking their hour-long nap.

Quickly and quietly everyone performed splendidly. Dad was the first to look out to the lawn and see the result. He woke up Mom and the two of them stood at the living room picture window looking out at all of us with tears in their eyes. We showed them the ad and they realized they better get dressed in their finest.

At two o'clock, hundreds of people descended onto the lawn each putting their single flower into a large basket. It became the world's largest bouquet by the end of the day.

Mom and Dad sat in two chairs while the crowd lined up and paid their respects. Dad's 100-year-old Uncle Charlie was there as well as every living relative and half of the town.

It was quite an event only to be surpassed by their move from Belle Plaine.

It's traumatic for elderly people to leave their home of many years and move into an assisted living environment. It was especially difficult for Mom and Dad to leave not only their home but also the town of Belle Plaine.

They agreed to move to a facility in Waconia, a town about 20 miles away. It would mean making new friends and shopping at new stores but more importantly leaving behind their old friends. They both dreaded moving day and were growing more morose as the final day approached. Dad was trying to keep a happy face to cheer a very unhappy Mom. She was upset and confused about how she could make the move and establish a new household. It seemed to overwhelm her. So we had a plan. If we could pull off the 65th anniversary trick why couldn't we move them in without her knowing? A complete move including soap under the sink and pictures on the wall...all within a brief period.

Mom and Dad watched as the truck with their things was loaded. My sister Karen was to drive them to Waconia along meandering back roads and take them to lunch on the way. The restaurant was instructed to come up with reasons why the service was slow. Karen was to drive slowly and take a few wrong turns.

Meanwhile, Terry, nephews Carl and David, daughters Kate and Molly and I were ready to meet the moving truck and flash into action. We went crazy finishing up the last touches as Karen drove up to the assisted living parking lot. As Mom and Dad walked through the door the last nail was pounded in, the last magazine was put in place and the last drawer was filled with their clothes.

Mother almost collapsed when she saw that her loving children and grandchildren had allayed her greatest fear. She sobbed almost uncontrollably.

It was a magical experience.

Tom Lynch loved a good story, was curious, couldn't read, never swore and built a successful business.

SOME REMEMBRANCES OF T.H.

Dear Old Dad

My dad's tiny office was under the steps to our apartment. It had two desks and a safe. One desk for Erma Schlingman, his 300-pound secretary, and one for him. I would go there and play insurance man and dig through his wastebasket for important-looking papers. The papers were often slimed with his tobacco spittle. My dad chewed cigars. What a mess.

Dad was a great shot. Once while fishing down at the river he overcast and snagged his lure in a tree on the other side. He wasn't going to lose that lucky lure. He had me hold the rod while he went home and got his 22-caliber rifle. A group of men gathered around and teased him about what a cheapskate he was (it's true) and bet him he couldn't shoot it down. He didn't aim at the lure. He found a point on the branch and hit the identical spot several times until the branch fell into the river and we could reel it in. I was proud of him that day.

I went with Mom and Dad to Sioux Lookout, Ontario on a luckless fishing trip. The Sioux Lookout was a long get at the end of the existing road system. It was so remote we were virtually guaranteed good luck. Yet we only caught a few hammer handle northerns. It was a Belle Plaine tradition to drive into town, park by the curb and open your trunk for everyone to see your catch. Right before Dad opened the trunk he whispered to me not to say a thing about what I was going to see. Much to my surprise, the trunk was filled with several 30-35 pound northerns. Dad had purchased them from some tribe members in Sioux Lookout. There were many oohs and aahs until Frank Johnson, the implement dealer from across the street, commented that the fish were headless. Usually, the heads were left on so the fish could be hung and photographed. Frank said that those must be Indian fish. Even though we didn't catch the fish, the fish caught Dad.

Dad was well known as a hunter and dog breeder in Belle Plaine. He had recently purchased two Weimaraners from a breeder. Dad billed the two as the best hunting dogs ever. They were a new breed from Germany and Dad wanted to show his fellow hunters how they would react. They went to a field and flushed up a pair of pheasants. Dad fired his 12-gauge twice and got both birds. The new dogs ran for cover and hid under the car rather than retrieving the birds. My embarrassed father had to drive the car off the dogs to get them in the trunk. He sold the dogs the next week.

He never wanted to be seen in a bar in Belle Plaine. It wouldn't be good if his dry Lutheran customers saw him there so he would have a few at home. He also couldn't be seen buying a bottle at the liquor store so he would drive 30 miles to Norwood, Minnesota and buy a case of Jim Beam. He hid it in the locked closet in the garage for fear that Uncle Gene might find it.

Everyone seemed to like my dad and he returned the love, except for any adult who acted poorly around kids. He would not tolerate swearing, drunkenness and rough behavior.

Dad wasn't a backslapping glad-hander either. He was always a big booster of Belle Plaine although he had trouble reading or giving a speech. I can remember him building and erecting a manger scene for Christmas that was placed on the side of Highway 169. He decorated the street lamps for Christmas and was chairman of the commercial club of Belle Plaine.

A mysterious person looking for land in Belle Plaine contacted him. That person was interested in tax breaks for a factory that would package fresh vegetables in a plastic pouch. The pouch could be thrown into boiling water. An amazing new concept at the time.

The town fathers wined and dined him as best they could when there were only three hamburger joints in town. He had a new Packard and wore a different suit each day they met him. Bob Anderson at the drugstore told the committee the stranger asked to use the phone in the back of the store and proceeded to call long distance using a credit card. A credit card for a phone call. "Can you believe that?" Bob exclaimed.

I was working at the drugstore at the time and heard all the town news. Suddenly, the stranger disappeared, never to be heard from again. Dad said he was a "four-flusher" trying to act big and get some attention and free meals. Everyone was devastated. Years later it was learned that he was from a company called Snoboy which eventually built a plant in Indiana. Dad tried to leverage that news into changes in the town. "We had no restaurants, no swimming pool and no golf course. Why would someone want to live in a town like Belle Plaine if you could build a plant anywhere in the US?" he said to his committee.

Dad was chairman of the big centennial celebration in Belle Plaine. It was a big deal and the biggest task he ever took on. He did a great job. I remember he grew a mustache for the event and got my mom to wear a 100-year-old dress and ride around town on a bicycle built for two. She would always sing, "Daisy, Daisy, give me your answer true, I'm just crazy all for the love of you." She was a good sport.

His civic participation must have rubbed off on me.

I heard from his friends how proud he was of me. He never mentioned a word.

He never swore.

He always knelt at his bedside and said his prayers. Mom did neither and was a good Presbyterian lady.

He was so remorseful when Mom died after 69 years of marriage.

He would break into tears when I visited him. He would lament that he didn't take her to New York or that he made her go fishing in Canada when he knew she hated it. A few weeks before he died, he looked at me and said he had an important question to ask me. He had been thinking a great deal about Judgment Day. He was certain that Mom would go to heaven even though she wasn't Catholic. "She was perfect," he always said.

His question dealt with the number of people going to heaven on the same day. Judgment Day. All the people since the beginning of time, even the cavemen. And all the people who would die years after he died. Billions of people rising up. I was worried that now, at this critical time, he was starting to lose his faith. That would be horrible. My fears were allayed when he looked up with his cloudy blue, misty eyes and said to me, "How will I find Ethel?" I assured him the creator had a plan for just that. That seemed to calm him.

Funny thing, I have never heard any other believer ask that same question.

Sorta with grandaughter Etta. Sorta Claus led the Holidazzle parade for ten years and made thousands of kids believe for another year.

SORTA CLAUS

Santa Has A Brother

DURING COLLEGE WHEN I CAME HOME for Christmas my dad would have me accompany him when he dropped off his annual business calendar to his best clients. I wore a Santa suit that was so shabby even the youngest/dumbest kid would know I was faking it. But I loved playing Santa. It was acting.

Years later, after I had established green as my favorite color, I had the Guthrie Theatre costume department make me a beautiful green velvet Santa suit, complete with bells on leather boots and a professional beard and wig. The outfit was so convincing people didn't know it was me.

I became Santa's brother, Sorta Claus. Santa in red, Sorta in green and sister Kinda in blue. While Santa liked good little girls, Sorta was less discriminating.

On Christmas Eve, Sorta would visit the Ronald McDonald House, Children's Hospital and several homes on Park Lane in Minneapolis. Playing Sorta wore me out.

Sorta also visited inner-city schools. The most unforgettable incident occurred after I finished telling the grade school children about my brother Santa and the singing of *Jingle Bells*. The teachers in the back of the room were giving me hand signals to extend my performance. They were going to bring other classes to see Sorta.

I had already told my standard story and the kids didn't want to sing anymore so I decided to encourage the kids to ask questions about my brother Santa.

It took a few minutes for someone brave enough to ask a question, but finally, a five-year-old from Somalia asked the first question. "What does Santa eat?" I blurted out the first thing that came to mind. "Raw cod and walrus hair," I said.

The next question came quickly. "Does Santa swear?" "No," I replied. "And if he did Father Christmas would bust his chops." While the kids were dumbfounded, the teachers in the back of the room were laughing their butts off.

"Did Santa know Jesus?" "Heck of a guy." Next question. And on it went. I only wish I had a video.

For several years Sorta Claus led the famous Holidazzle parade downtown. It was exhilarating going down Nicollet Mall lit up with bright Christmas lights, music and thousands of kids in wonder.

I was happy my young grandkids were on that first float with me.

Sorta slowed down. 2018 was the last time he suited up. Sorta has probably gone back to the North Pole to be with Kinda.

HEAD IN THE GAME

He's Out!

LOU BACIG MY BUSINESS PARTNER FOR UMPTEEN YEARS at Carmichael Lynch, was one hell of a baseball player. Threw right, batted left and was close to semi-pro. He was a catcher and known for trash-talking the batter while crowding him.

Crowding the batter has some pitfalls. Sometimes you get hit, either by the bat or the ball. The story goes that Lou got decked by a bat while playing at Midway Field in St. Paul.

A fastball came in low. The batter chopped down at it catching Lou's catcher's mask at the brim and forcing his head down. The batter missed the ball and it connected with the top of Lou's exposed head knocking him out. Lou fell face forward on the plate while the game went on.

The ball looked and sounded like a bunt so the ball was in play. Lou, dead to the world, was stepped on by a man coming from third to score.

Lou was taken to the hospital with a concussion.

I wasn't sure this story was true until I ran into a friend of Lou's who played in the same game. It was.

Lou was always intense. No matter what, he kept his head in the game.

Inventor Edgar Hetteen in Alaska sitting on one of his first snowmobiles and a more recent model.

EDGAR

An Inventive Mind

EDGAR HETTEEN WAS AN AMAZING MAN. He was born and raised among the jack pines near Roseau, Minnesota, close to the US border with Canada. Edgar barely finished grade school and became an apprentice at a local farm implement repair shop. He loved bending metal and figuring out how things worked. His first invention was a straw chopper and, while not a commercial success, it was the gateway to several other inventions, including the first snowmobile. Edgar was the Leonardo da Vinci of the frozen tundra.

Edgar, with his brother Allan, manufactured a prototype of the first snowmobile. It was long and heavy, noisy, uncomfortable and could not travel in more than five inches of snow or climb more than a 20% grade. But it was the beginning of a huge industry.

The Hetteen brothers found some financial backing and started Polaris Industries. The machine got lighter, stronger and slowly started to resemble the machine of today.

Edgar was not getting along with Allan so he moved down the road to Thief River Falls, Minnesota and started Arctic Cat. He made snowmobiling famous in 1968 by becoming the first person to travel the Yukon River in Alaska in the dead of winter. The lack of good cold-weather gear and a dependable machine made the trip treacherous but he reached the Bering Sea and his adventure appeared in *Sports Illustrated.*

Arctic Cat became a larger company and in 1971 went public to become the fastest-growing company on the New York Stock Exchange. Edgar was the founder and the president was an accountant from town, Lowell Swenson. The day before the company went public Edgar and I were in Lowell's office when Lowell took a phone call from a broker saying he had a few thousand unsold shares. The market had closed for the day and he couldn't find a buyer. The stock was to go public at 9 a.m. the following day. Lowell asked if I would like to buy them at the low pre-public offering rate. Being a stock market novice at that time, I didn't know he was offering me thousands of dollars. The shares could be sold the next day for 20 times my cost. I passed, thinking I had to come up with cash in the next few days. In those days I didn't have a pot to pee in and missed a big opportunity. Had I held the stock for five years it would have been worth over a million dollars. Ouch.

Edgar didn't have a lot of stock in the company he founded. He sold most of his for pennies trying to keep the company afloat. But money didn't interest him. The excitement of being to Arctic Cat what Willie Davidson was to Harley Davidson drove him. Edgar was chief engineer although he never went to a day of engineering school.

Edgar loved the people he worked with and loved the rural pioneering snowmobiler more than anyone. He became a roving ambassador and the darling of the media traveling the world of snow on four continents.

Edgar was pushed into the background as professional managers came into this almost billion-dollar company. He continued to invent and blaze new trails.

We became close friends. He counted on me to help him with new ideas and invest in new startup companies. I would do anything for Edgar. He gave me my first big break in advertising in 1968. Edgar hired me because his current ad agency was a one-man shop and could not keep up with the growth of the company. Edgar did not talk to the big agencies in town after a mutual friend arranged a meeting with Carmichael Lynch.

Edgar asked me to fly to Thief River and meet him at the American Legion Club. He asked me what I drank and I replied, "Scotch and soda." The waitress soon came back with two drinks for each of us. As we finished one another appeared. Edgar liked my small-town background and apparently something else because at breakfast the next morning I was hired. Arctic was just taking off and Edgar and I went on the ride of our lives.

Edgar's first wife attempted suicide eight times and succeeded on the ninth. It screwed up the lives of his children and caused many sad moments even after Edgar married his wife's sister, Hannah. I loved Hannah. The three of us shared many wonderful business trips together.

At age 75 Edgar and his old friend Gary Lemke started a tracked vehicle company called All Season Vehicle, ASV. The company went public and I joined its board of directors. The vehicle was first designed to groom snowmobile trails. It morphed into a work vehicle with multiple uses because its superior track system enabled it to float on soft or muddy ground. The company grew, eventually selling to the public company Terex. Edgar made his first big money. He had always quit and moved on to other inventions in the past. Terry and I also did very well.

In September 2009, Terry and I visited Edgar in a nursing home in Grand Rapids on our way to visit my sister Karen. I was shocked and saddened to see that Edgar's mind was ravaged by Alzheimer's. He looked at me closely and I thought he recognized me. Alas, he asked if I was a medic. It broke my heart. I had failed to visit him the year before when he was healthy and living at his home. I will never forget that terrible omission.

Bill Torp

David Bennett

Paddy McDevit

DEATH AND DYING

Good Friends

AS WE AGE WE HAVE MORE OPPORTUNITIES to observe the process of dying. Having been spared the horrors of war and calamity I have had only limited exposure to the act of dying. Here are some memories.

BILL TORP

Everyone respected and liked my brother-in-law Bill Torp, MD. I was lucky to have a brother-in-law as a good friend and an ad hoc medical advisor.

Bill was diagnosed with leukemia at the height of his career as chief of the medical staff at Abbott Northwestern Hospital. Bill was able to practice for another year. Then as weakness overcame his ability to go to the office, he worked for insurance companies on claims while at home. Bill often commented on how disappointed he was with many doctors and the charges for services they demanded.

Bill was finally too weak to work. He did not want to die in a hospital or have any life-extending procedures. His final days were spent at home with his family and in his own bed.

We took turns sitting up with Bill as his final hours approached. I happened to be on duty in his last hours. Even though he was only hours away from death he still felt the urge to urinate.

I picked him up in my arms (he was only skin and bones) to put him on the toilet. As I approached the bowl I slipped on some water and fell. Not wanting to hurt Bill, I twisted my body so that I would hit the floor first. Unfortunately I fell between the wall and the toilet bowl with Bill on top of me. I was wedged in and had a hard time getting out without hurting him even more. He knew the moment was chaotic but managed to say, "Lynch, you bastard." Those were his last words. He died a few hours later.

I don't think he meant it. Or did he?

DAVID BENNETT

I was lucky to have an attorney for 30 plus years who was also one of my best friends. Carmichael Lynch hired Dave as a young lawyer with the firm Gray Plant Mooty. I liked him because he represented a photo gallery which permitted people to come in with their own cameras and take pictures of nude women. Weird. David took the case pro bono as a free speech issue and won. My kind of lawyer.

Through the years Dave and I met monthly so I could keep him up to date on issues – real estate, stock plans, expansions. He would refer some issues to other firms if he felt that no one at Gray Plant was up to the task. I liked that. My partner Lou and I were good customers because of our real estate deals (most of them complicated). A 15% interest in the Sheraton Ritz hotel before it was condemned (we did OK, not great). Our purchase of a series of old mansions from the Minneapolis Institute of Arts. The purchase of 800 Hennepin Avenue and then 730 Hennepin Avenue. The most complicated deal by far was setting up our Employee Stock Ownership Plan (ESOP). It was an unusual plan at the time but worked well, especially for the employees who hung in there until we sold to IPG.

I got Dave to invest in our famous movie, *It Ain't Easy*. He never complained about losing his $25K. We skied together frequently. He was always in the lead with me trailing far behind. He introduced me to heli-skiing in the Bugaboos.

Dave, like Bill Torp, was diagnosed with leukemia and had a slow decline. He stayed active as long as he could and skied with 102° fever six weeks before he died.

I was able to talk to Dave in the hospital while he was getting a blood transfusion, his last. We recalled the good times, the scary times and the deals we worked on together. I told him I never saw his bills. I asked our CFO simply to pay them. Dave said that was extremely uncommon in the business and he appreciated it. It probably caused him not to bill for certain meetings.

I left after an hour as he was getting weaker. I knew that was going to be the last time I saw my dear friend. He died in September.

On October 1st, I got a bill for one hour of consulting…$500.

What a great sense of humor.

A REAL IRISH WAKE

My dad called me at the University and asked me to come home to Belle Plaine the coming Friday. Although I had plans I knew whatever he was calling about must be serious.

Dad wanted me to attend an authentic Irish wake to be held on a farm about five miles from town. He thought this might be one of the last of its kind. Paddy McDevit died at the age of 103 and the wake (as it was called) would be a big event.

When we arrived at the farm about 9:30 that evening there were dozens of cars and two tractors in the farmyard and pasture. The farmhouse had long narrow screen porches on two sides packed with men standing shoulder to shoulder and talking in low tones.

As my dad stepped up to the porch he was offered a sip from a bottle that was being passed around. It never got to me. He told me it was a tradition. We went into the kitchen where at least ten women were preparing food. I never got to the dining room where the food was served.

My dad was in a hurry to see old Paddy before the rosary started. A rosary was said on the hour throughout the night. If you were in the viewing room you were expected to get down on your knees and pray the rosary which took about 20 minutes.

There was Paddy, in a coffin propped up 45 degrees and holding a well smoked pipe in his hand. He was almost sitting up. I remember the odd smell, the many candles and the low ceiling. It was weird. Dad and I knelt and said a quick prayer while watching Paddy. A few people came up behind us and commented on how good Paddy looked, how natural.

A couple men who knew dad stopped him to talk and take another sip. He stayed a bit too long. Father Minouge came in and asked dad to kneel with him during the rosary. Darn, we were trapped for another 20 minutes right next to Paddy.

I would swear he had a glass eye and was looking at me.

BIRTHDAY SURPRISES

Creative Fun

OVER THE YEARS I have been fortunate to have friends and loved ones plan big birthday events for me.

FORTY

The agency planned a highly creative 40th. I was awakened at 7 a.m. by the Richfield High School marching band coming down the street and then filing into my house playing the *Stars and Stripes Forever*. I thought that was it. Wrong!

A man with an accordion was standing in my parking spot as I pulled into the underground parking area. As I got out of my car, he started playing *Lady of Spain*. I tried to talk to him but every time I spoke, he would start *Lady* all over again. As I walked to the elevator he played. As I went to my office he played. If I sat still, he would sit still. If I talked, he played. Phone. Talk. He played. I was starting to tire of the joke and offered to buy him out. He replied while playing *Lady* that if

I made an offer my friends would match it.

While on the phone, a woman in a raincoat came into my office and asked if I was 40? I said yes and she opened her raincoat and proudly showed herself off and said, "I'm forty too, get it?" She left quickly. I was disappointed that the manager of the production department had arranged something so tacky.

I thought I could shake the accordionist when I went to lunch with an old friend who was not connected to the agency. I met John Davidson at the Sofitel restaurant. John was waiting for me with the accordion player. He was in on the plot. I tried to talk to John but the damn accordion drowned me out. It also drowned out other customers and conversations. The manager (who was not in on the gag) escorted the accordion player and me out the door. We had a birthday cake and beer at the end of the day. I was glad to go home and relax. I was exhausted. I went to my bedroom, opened the door, and the accordion player was playing one last burst of *Lady of Spain*.

FIFTY

Late in the afternoon of my birthday I was physically removed from my office in the Pillsbury mansion and placed on a flatbed trailer pulled by a truck. I had to wear a cloak and crown and was the feature of a half block-long parade. Music, majorettes and spectators lined the sidewalks. We entered the auditorium of the Women's Club and were treated to a great performance by Vern Sutton and Janis Hardy, of the Minnesota Opera Company, and my good friend Philip Brunelle. They took ideas from the audience and did a fabulous improv to tunes from Bizet's *Carmen*. It was great.

SIXTY

The highlight of my 60th was the recording of a song I wrote called *Ants in the Pants*. Son-in-law Chris Beaty wrote music to the lyrics and the kids and grandkids sang. The song was debuted at a nice surprise party at the Minikahda Club. Then on to Portugal and an amazing bedroom fit for a king.

The big 60th was Terry's. I arranged for the billboard on top of

Bravo Restaurant on Hennepin Avenue in downtown Minneapolis to proclaim, "Saario is 60." Janis, a limo driver we frequently used, picked her up at home and drove her down 9th street so she could see the full effect of the billboard. When Terry walked into the restaurant she found the first floor packed with friends and the Bravo Broadway singers belting out favorite tunes. On cue they started to sing to the tune of *Mama Mia*, "Terra Mia, uh oh up we go"… and we all went to the second floor.

An St. Paul Chamber Orchestra string quartet performed on the second floor. The walls were decorated with wonderful blowup photos of Terry over the years. They were breathtaking. A highlight of the second floor was an idea from daughters Kate and Molly. Everyone was asked to write a memory of Terry on a 3"x 5" card and hang it on a memory tree that had been pasted to the wall. It was a wonderful and loving idea.

After some toasts, good wine and a great lamb dinner, we progressed to the third floor (another "Terra Mia, uh oh got to go"…) where Chris Beaty and a great band played all of Terry's favorite hits from The Band, James Taylor, the Beatles and others. I sang on bended knee, "Will you still love me, will you still need me when I'm 64?" As of this writing, I am 84 and she still loves me.

SEVENTY

Terry went crazy on my 70th. It started with an auction at the annual St. Paul Chamber Orchestra gala. A company offered the use of its corporate jet overnight to Chicago as an auction item. It turned out no one was interested in overnighting in Chicago. After an awkward period of no bidding, Terry asked if the owner would change the offer to an overnight anywhere in the US. Because of the noise in the room not everyone heard the change in the offer. Terry did and swooped in and got the jet overnight to Napa Valley.

We booked four rooms at Meadowood Resort and invited our good friends Sam and Lisa, Rosanne and Mike, and Connie and Theresa to join us. Terry arranged for Savories restaurant to cater a special breakfast on the plane. Sam brought a case of wine from Minnesota to Napa (that's a switch) and impressed the sommelier at the exclusive Auberge restaurant in Napa that evening, croquet in the morning in the obligatory whites, and then off to lunch at a hot spot called Red where our dear friend, the Honorable Thelton P. Henderson, joined us. Back to the plane, more good wine and in bed by at ten. What a birthday!

EIGHTY

My eightieth was a family-only party in Florida. We rented a huge home on the water near Fort Myers. Everyone, including brand new great-grand-baby Benjamin and our Antiguan son Lawson, came down for the event. Great cooking by everyone except Terry and me (we weren't allowed in the kitchen), beach time, many games and elegant hanging out.

My big 80th gift was a fine green ukulele. I had always wanted a good uke. Daughter Kate arranged for 16 small ukes for everyone else. I was very pleasantly surprised when everyone took out their ukes. Chris Beaty taught everyone four cords and we all played old songs for most of the night. My fingers were sore.

NINETY

Pudding, cake and ice cream at the assisted living facility. None of the kids came.

ONE HUNDRED

Just Terry and me in hospice. I wish she would stop telling me to stand up straight.

Accordionist Larry Poehl followed me everywhere from 7 a.m. to 10 p.m. I now hate Lady of Spain.

Might have been the world's shortest parade.

Poster of a young Terry, surrounded by musicians from the St. Paul Chamber Orchestra.

Lonnie Hammergren, M.D.

LONNIE

Las Vegas Kitsch

Dr. lonnie hammergren, a psychiatrist from Rush City, Minnesota had an incredibly unique home in Las Vegas. As you entered, mounted on one wall was an odd species of goat. The animal grew a second set of horns that curved backward and inward into the animal's eye, eventually killing it.

Lonnie and I were classmates at Chi Psi fraternity, both of us from small towns and both our fathers were insurance men. Lonnie breezed through pre-med in two years and medical school as fast. He was a tried-and-tested genius eventually earning five degrees. He was the flight surgeon for the 1st Airborne in Vietnam, completing over a hundred helicopter missions earning a purple heart.

He moved on to become the flight surgeon for the Apollo Space program before getting his degree in neurosurgery. He practiced at the Mayo Clinic for two years and earned his psychiatry diploma before departing for Las Vegas to become the only neurosurgeon in the city.

Lonnie claims to have worked on more boxers and motorcycle victims than anyone in the country.

Lonnie was an active citizen serving on many boards. He eventually ran for and was elected lieutenant governor of Nevada.

Lonnie was a collector. He focused on Las Vegas history, signs, and props from shows as well as many items from the NASA space program, including a scale model of the lunar landing vehicle. The artifacts he amassed over the years spilled out onto his front lawn...like the fuselage of an F15 fighter. That's when he started receiving collection notices. To satisfy potential lawsuits from the neighbors he bought the two adjacent homes, connected them and filled all three homes with thousands of items.

I visited Lonnie in March 2013. Three different cab drivers knew where Dr. Hammergren lived and said he was crazy. Lonnie's eccentric behavior was well known.

He hugged me at the door. We walked into the living room where he played a tune on Liberace's piano. He then escorted me, for three hours, through over one hundred rooms and three rooftops.

Lonnie looked old and shuffled around the building. He had trouble getting up many steps. Everything was a mess. In each room he would pick up something he felt was out of place, tell me a story about it and say he had to work in this room next week. He said that about every room. The place was falling apart. He had no help in maintaining this huge collection.

He seemed like a crazy old man lost in his stuff and memories. I knew he was off the deep end when he took me to a sub-basement and showed me the crypt he planned to be buried in.

I smiled when he took me to his bedroom. The room had an oversized round bed with a large dome in the ceiling above it. The dome was painted blue with twinkling stars. It depicted the northern sky in Rush City on December 25, 1937, the day Lonnie was born.

Lonnie was heartbroken when museums rejected his collection. He finally went bankrupt and died in 2009.

SNOWSPORTS DIGEST

lights...camera...action (good and bad)

WORLD PREMIERE IT AIN'T EASY

FALLS

It Ain't Easy

The big night — the world premiere of "It Ain't Easy" at the Falls in Thief River Falls, Minnesota.

The past few years, there have been movies like "Easy Rider" and "Evil Knievel" that revolve around motorcycles. Then there have been movies such as "Grand Prix" and "LeMans" that involve cars and racing. And there have been movies like "Snow Job" and "Downhill Racer" that center around skiing. Now there is a full length feature movie involving snowmobiles. The title is: "It Ain't Easy."

"It Ain't Easy" isn't likely to win any academy awards, particularly for acting or plot. But if you are a snowmobiler, you should see it, if for no other reason than that it contains some of the best snowmobile photography ever shot.

It is not surprising that the snowmobiling and snowmobile photography is perhaps the highlight of the movie. The people who originally planned It Ain't Easy, the people who filmed it, the snowmobile drivers and, in fact, the people who financed it and provided a lot of other help are all snowmobilers.

For example, Maurice Hurley, the director and producer, is an avid snowmobiler who has been involved in snowmobile photography for several years, primarily for an advertising agency. The technical advisor for the movie is Charlie Lofton, a former race team captain for Arctic Cat. The stunt drivers on snowmobiles, in addition to Lofton, are Paul Eggebraaten and Larry Colton, members of the Arctic Cat factory racing team. A couple of the actors are employees of Arctic Cat. And the world premiere of the movie was held in Thief River Falls, Minnesota. That happens to be the home town of a large snowmobile manufacturing company. Guess which one.

So the movie draws on a lot of snowmobile experience, and the driving and snowmobile photography show it. The music is good, too. But other than that, highlights are hard to find.

The story centers around Randy Sorensen, who is just discharged from military service and has spent time "on the road" roaming the country. Randy decides he can best find himself by returning to his home in northern Minnesota (Located, coincidentally, just outside Thief River Falls). Expecting to find peace and a simple way of life, Randy instead finds changes and trouble. First,

The world premier in Thief River Falls, MN.
Maury at the trout weighing station near Sitka, Alaska.

MAURY HURLEY

Newsman, Producer, Writer, Hustler and Friend

GETTING FIRED WITH DRAMA

Maury was a lead news producer at KSTP television in the Twin Cities. At the time KSTP was the leading news station in the Cities and owned by an ultra-conservative. Maury hated the owner who put his imprint on the news in almost every show. He especially didn't like his political point of view. He had finally had enough and decided to quit...no, get fired in a Hurley flame.

It was the tenth anniversary of the most celebrated murder in the state, the murder of the wife of T. Eugene Thompson, attorney and lover boy. Thompson hired a hitman from Chicago to do the ugly deed. The hitman broke into their home in St. Paul and stabbed her. She managed to crawl down the staircase on her stomach leaving a trail of blood on the steps and in a pool on the landing where she succumbed.

Maury learned T. Eugene was due to appear in a talent show at the state penitentiary singing *Someday I'll Find You*. Maury filmed T. Eugene singing while intercutting the song with scenes of the bloody murder.

Maury knew the station owner would be watching the show and sold chances on how long it would take before he rang the newsroom and fired Maury. Fourteen minutes.

Maury then joined Carmichael Lynch to form a film subsidiary. The fun began.

MAURY THE HUSTLER

He didn't look like a golfer. That impression helped him hustle money on the golf course.

We were both in Montana working on a project and took an afternoon off to golf. I borrowed a friend's clubs and glove while Maury rented an odd assortment of old clubs. Maury insisted that we bet a hundred dollars on the game (more than I have ever bet before or after). We both did poorly on the first three holes. I realized Maury was as bad a golfer as I was. I pulled ahead by five strokes. With five holes to play, rain broke out making the mountainous course slippery. Maury insisted on doubling the bet. I decided to take it and teach him a lesson. Five strokes, rain, slipping and sliding, weird clubs, no glove…I couldn't miss.

He won by one stroke. If he had lost he would have had to pay me later. He didn't have the cash to cover the bet. I got hustled.

It Ain't Easy… AND IT WASN'T

CL was making award-winning commercials for Harley-Davidson motorcycles and Arctic Cat snowmobiles as well as other products. How hard could it be to make a movie? It's just like stringing 90 commercials together, right?

The movie rage at the time was motorcycle crime. Hell's Angels movies. Cheap thrillers.

The newly emerging sub-culture of snowmobilers loved to see snow machines race, crash and splash around in the snow. We could film this and simply follow the formula of the motorcycle movies. A race, a rape and a crash. Easy!

Maury wrote a script. We had panels drawn to depict the scenes…

the same way we sold commercials. People seem to need to see a picture even if it's a cartoon drawing. It was cumbersome to show panel after panel illustrating the script as we made presentations to potential investors. To make it easier we attached all the panels to a rope and hung the rope in the presentation. It looked like laundry hanging on a clothesline.

We slowly raised the $500,000 needed to go into production.

Maury was everywhere doing everything including acting in a small part.

We thought we were going to hit it big when the bible of the film industry, *American Cinematographer*, featured our movie on its cover bumping off a Gene Hackman movie called *The French Connection.* We were going to make millions!

Until the story didn't work. We could tell early on that we had a mess on our hands.

To save money we filmed one of the scenes in the bedroom of my house. A yellow bedroom. Everything was lemon yellow. Walls, carpet, bedspread, furniture. Bright lemon yellow.

I thought it would be a quick shoot so I didn't tell my wife at the time how involved it would be. Little did she (or I) know that a utility pole would be dug in our front lawn and a huge van parked in the street for three days.

Our three kids, (4, 8, and 9), ate breakfast each morning while they watched the star getting make up in our kitchen. They loved it. My wife was furious.

A major investor in the film was the Arctic Cat company located in Thief River Falls, a small town in northern Minnesota. To honor the company we decided to hold the premiere there and fly in press and investors. This was a big deal for a small town. Movie stars. Searchlights. Red carpet. A limo dropped the stars off in front of the recently painted theater and circled to the back of the theater to pick up the next star.

The movie was DOA. No applause even on your home turf. It received perhaps the worst review ever given by the *Minneapolis Star Tribune.* The last line of the review was telling. "Lynch and Hurley should stick to making commercials."

Unfortunately it ran on the big screen in Minneapolis for three weeks, embarrassing the hell out of me. It also ran in 55 other markets and managed to lose money in every one of them. We had a critical and financial failure. *It Ain't Easy* was not only hard to watch but even harder to think about.

Maury was humiliated and left town for LA. He swore he would never direct or produce again–just write. And a writer he was.

Maury kept himself alive by golf hustling. Through golf, Maury met Don Johnson, the star of *Miami Vice*, a hot series worldwide. Don liked Maury and gave him a shot at writing for the show. Over the next few years a third of *Miami Vice* scripts were written by Maury.

He went on to write for *Star Trek, The Next Generation* and became the executive producer. He hired Whoopi Goldberg which turned out to be great for the show.

And a writer he was. I had lunch with Maury in LA in 2006. He met me at one of the most elite golf clubs in LA. Maury had come a long way from Maury the hustler to Maury the country club guy.

FISHING WITH MAURY

Miami Vice got Maury on a solid financial footing so he could enjoy life a bit. Relax? Wrong. Maury couldn't relax even while fishing. On a fishing trip to Alaska he had to complete a script for *Kojak*, the TV show starring Telly Savalas. He was hired as a script doctor to solve a problem. The star of the show was in an advanced stage of dementia. Savalas was unable to remember a line or even read a prompter. All the shots of him had to be away from his face and his lines were dubbed in.

Maury was late in delivering the script. He had to write in the boat during bad weather. Each night the producers yelled at him for not being finished. This went on for the five days we were in Alaska. I said, "Maury, this isn't much fun for me. I came to talk. You're always writing." Maury replied, "You didn't come on a talking trip. You came on a fishing trip. So fish."

Maury died in 2016 of a heart attack. He was 75 years old. Terry and I went to the funeral. What a crowd–everyone from William Shatner to Whoopi Goldberg and a hundred others.

HEAVY METAL

Nephew Eric

My sister Karen had three boys, Eric, Carl and David. Eric was born with a troubling growth on his cheek and it affected him in many ways. He was a good kid, small for his age and hyperactive. I found it easier to connect with Carl and David. As Eric got older music became a possible connection to him.

As the head of a firm in a "hip" industry, I went out of my way to stay on top of trends and to experience, among other phenomena, the music culture of the moment.

I mentioned to Eric that I had tickets to a heavy metal concert at the Met Center and wanted to know if he would like to go. Twisted Sister and Iron Maiden were performing. Eric found it amazing I would want to hear the meanest, loudest, and most vulgar sounds of the day. I told him I would pick him up at 7 p.m. and I would be coming from work. He asked me what I would be wearing. I said my normal suit and bow tie. Eric groaned and told me to change. I told him I didn't have time. He pleaded with me. He said I could cause trouble looking so straight. I told him not to worry.

When I picked him up he surprised me by wearing a suit and a tie. Wow. As we mingled in the crowd before the show started we could hear the grungers whispering, "Shhhh, there's a narc."

The concert was painful to my eyes and ears. Firecrackers shot off. One number did me in. The lyrics were "If you hate your mother, stand up and stomp." Virtually everyone got up and stomped. Searchlights scanned the room for holdouts and, with the help of surrounding fans, the searchlights found this guy sitting down. Me!

In the glare of the searchlight, I stood up and stomped just to get the light off me. It was a low moment in my life.

Forgive me, Mom, I love you.

DINNER WITH THE BOYS

Double Death Dessert

TERRY WAS OUT OF TOWN so I thought it would be nice to have my dad and brother Tommy to the cabin. Dad needed perking up. He was heartbroken since my mom's death.

I served them steak and corn on the cob and then went into the kitchen to prepare dessert.

My dad shouted, "Lee, Lee, come here quickly." I ran out on the deck and could tell Tommy was choking on something, probably steak. Even though it was dusk I could see a blue tinge to his skin. Tommy was always at risk of choking because of his cerebral palsy.

I lifted him out of the chair, wrapped my arms around him and gave a huge squeeze. The steak burst out of his mouth with a cork popping sound. Unfortunately his false teeth also came out, slid across the deck and dropped down into the ravine. I grabbed a flashlight and started searching. I had just found the teeth when my dad called out again.

"Lee, Lee, come quick. My nitroglycerin. Quick!" My God, he was having a heart attack. I instantly searched the pockets in his floppy slacks but came up empty. He kept saying, "Hurry, hurry."

I ran into the bedroom to check his toilet kit. Nothing. Then the bathroom. No nitro. Dad was now panicked and in pain.

I searched his pockets again and found the tiny vial in the corner of his pocket. Thank God! It gave him instant relief.

I went back into the kitchen and held onto the counter. My head was spinning. My God, my father and brother almost died at the same time. I pulled myself together and went out to see how they were doing.

They both wanted to know what was for dessert. "Dessert? Dessert? You both almost died and you can only think of dessert?"

Son and father waiting for dinner.

Joe and Rose are still married.

JOE AND ROSE

Love Letter

I MET JOE SELVAGGIO IN 1965 shortly after he ended his "death walk" around the Federal Building in downtown Minneapolis, dressed in Dominican robes, with a white plastered face representing death. This was Joe's way of bearing witness against the war in Vietnam. It was also a good way to end his priesthood and become a full-time advocate for peace and an agent against poverty and racism.

Joe, through St. Joan of Arc parish, found 100 good souls to contribute $5 a month for his upkeep. In exchange he became your advocate on social justice issues and published a quarterly and annual report.

During this period, he met and married an unlikely woman, raucous Phoebe Kane, a former nun. It was his first dalliance. They adopted two disabled Hispanic boys and then had their son, Sam. Joe and Phoebe divorced but remain friends.

A few years later a friend and priest from the Philippines contacted Joe. His friend was concerned about the life and possible freedom of one of his parishioners who was a leader in the anti-Marcos effort. He wanted to get Rose Escanan out of the country before she was uncovered by the Marcos regime. She could immigrate to the US only if she were to be married and could show evidence a groom was waiting for her.

He asked Joe to start writing love letters to Rose so she could respond. I helped Joe compose some of the letters which turned out to be harder than one might imagine.

After a few months, officials in Manila were convinced the romance was real and granted Rose permission to depart...only she didn't have enough money for airfare.

We organized a fundraiser at my office in the old Pillsbury mansion. Almost 100 people attended, including about twenty individuals from the local Philippine community. They brought delicious indigenous foods to the party and we raised enough money for the ticket.

My dear mother Ethel, who was tight with the dollar, gave $25 to the cause. When asked why she contributed she said Joe had visited her almost every day when she was in the hospital.

Rose arrived. They were married before a justice of the peace. What happened next? You guessed it. Joe and Rose fell in love and were married again a year later.

As a wedding gift, they returned everyone's contribution for her ticket. My mother could not believe she got back a check for $25. She refused to cash it.

Chieu Nghiem on his wedding day.

CHIEU

An Immigrant's Story

CHIEU NGHIEM CAME TO OUR FAMILY shortly after Saigon fell at the end of the Vietnam War. I had been vehemently opposed to the war and believed taking a refugee into my life was the least I could do in reparation for all the harm we caused the Vietnamese.

I was informed by Catholic Charities, the sponsoring organization, that a teenager was going to get off a plane at approximately 1 a.m. That night I went to the airport. No teen or Vietnamese got off the plane. Two other prospective foster fathers and I returned home and went again the next night. Still no teens. However a large Vietnamese family got off the plane, walked into the vacant airport lobby and squatted down in the middle of the floor. Not a soul in sight except me. I asked them if I could help and realized they didn't speak any English.

I wondered if they needed to use the bathroom so I pointed to my pants and the father of the family nodded yes. I took them to the toilet but found they did not want to be divided. The women wanted to stay with the father and use the men's room. I realized they didn't know how to use the toilets.

We all assembled again in the lobby. I tried to put them into two different cabs since there were nine of them. The father would not allow his family to be separated presenting a bit of a dilemma. Luckily I knew the manager of the airport Sheraton Hotel. I called the night clerk asking to use their airport van. He cleared the request. Soon a driver showed up, piled all of the family into the van and followed me home.

The entire family slept on my living room floor (Mary, my then wife, and the kids were in Mexico). The next morning I called my neighbor David Lykken and invited him and his wife for breakfast with me and a few friends. They were surprised when they saw nine bodies lying on the carpet sound asleep. I made rice and scrambled eggs.

Later Lutheran Social Services arrived and connected them with a sponsoring family. I wonder how they did in America.

On the third night three teens got off the plane. The three of us pointed arbitrarily to one of the teens. "I'll take that one." "You take that one." Off we went. Chieu didn't speak English and had no baggage –only a life preserver from a boat and a small paper bag with airplane food neatly wrapped in it.

I immediately started to teach him English using stop lights as the cue. Red...go, green...stop. I did that about 15 times on the way home stopping at every light. He seemed to understand. Later in life he told me he had no idea what I was talking about.

After about five months Chieu started acting strangely. There was a great deal of violence in the public school where the city placed refugees in. Chieu would come home badly bruised and scratched. He had to fight Laotians, Thais or Cambodians. Ancient animosities followed them to Minnesota. The school soon realized they had to separate the different nationalities. That solved the problem. Chieu was given to angry outbursts. He was skilled in martial arts and our children felt threatened when he got upset. I didn't believe my kids until I experienced his wrath.

I was on a phone attached to the wall near the kitchen when Chieu came storming up the basement stairs. His face was bright red. I told him to be quiet and was shocked when he raised his foot and thrust it at my head. He wasn't aiming for my head but sheared the phone off the wall to send me a message.

The University of Minnesota had a Chinese speaking psychiatrist. He noted that many immigrants from violent countries have the equivalent of nervous breakdowns about the same time Chieu experienced his. The doctor helped Chieu through his trauma but I had to get him out of the house.

A social service agency found him a room with a single woman about a mile from us. I visited Chieu and slowly realized something was not right with his living arrangement. It turns out that she was taking advantage of him. He felt terrible about even bringing it up to me. We had him relocated again and the predator was taken off of all foster housing lists.

Chieu's life jacket had a special place in his life. To this day it sits above his fireplace at home. It turns out Chieu escaped twice from Vietnam. The first time his small boat was captured by pirates. They tortured Chieu to find out where he hid his gold. He will forever have the scars from the electrodes on both of his biceps.

His second attempt ended in a swamped boat. Rather than going back to shore and possible incarceration or torture he swam out into the South China Sea as many escapees did over those years. Most drowned.

Chieu was spotted at dusk by a freighter flying a foreign flag. He was hauled up on board. As the hoist pulled him overboard it slipped and slammed his body into the side of the ship breaking his leg. That turned out to be a lucky break. Rather than being sent to the camps in Thailand for a prolonged stay he was sent to a hospital in Hong Kong. Chieu was savvy enough to get a refugee organization to fly him out of Hong Kong.

Chieu thought he was in Ireland when he arrived in Minnesota. The relocation program was chaotic.

Chieu graduated from Holy Angels Academy along with my son Chris. He married Ling Chou, who survived the killing fields of Cambodia.

He bought a home in Bloomington and paid it off in ten years. Chieu and Ling raised two kids, Amy and George.

A happy and sad incident in their lives (and ours) was Chieu's desire to get his mother, three sisters and two brothers from Saigon to Minnesota. He sent $5,000 for plane tickets and after a long wait we received word they were on their way. We worked hard to prepare Chieu's home for six more occupants.

Our friends contributed clothes and furniture. We partitioned off small cells in his basement so that everyone had some privacy. It was tight.

An incredibly emotional moment occurred when his family got off the plane and embraced Chieu. We all cried. It had taken almost ten years but they were finally in Minneapolis.

It didn't take longer than a week for the first major conflict to erupt. In the Chinese culture the mother controls the house and is the head of the household. Ling, now westernized, would not let go and the issue reached a climax when Chieu was forced to choose between his mother and his wife.

The family not only moved out but dissed Chieu in the Chinese community. Being disowned by your family was serious and it affected many of Chieu's friendships. It took another ten years for reconciliation.

Later while on a trip to Vietnam, my wife Terry and I learned it was taboo for a Vietnamese man to marry a Cambodian woman.

Ling died in June of 2021.

9/11

WRONG PLACE, WRONG TIME

A Week in Central Park

TERRY AND I WERE ON VACATION with friends in Maine and planned to go from there to New York City where I was scheduled to make a speech to the Outdoor Advertising Association. I had to cut my vacation short and get back to Minneapolis for a day. So our plans changed. I was to meet Terry at Logan Airport in Boston and go on from there to New York.

My flight from Minneapolis to Boston arrived late and I was going to miss connecting with Terry for our flight to New York. As I departed the Northwest plane we were met by a small shuttle to transfer us to the terminal. I gave the shuttle driver $20 to drop me off by the ladder going up to the American plane. Illegal but he did it.

The flight was about to take off and Terry was still at the gate anxiously waiting for me. A gate attendant rushed to her and told her the flight was ready to leave. She needed to get on the plane. Her husband was already in his seat. The scene at Logan was chaotic but Terry could not figure out how she had missed me.

We stayed at our usual place, The Phillips Club, right next to Lincoln Center. We like it because of its location and roominess–it has a kitchen, TV room and king size bedroom.

On the morning of September 11, 2001, we had breakfast at a small diner before heading to the Carmichael Lynch PR office in midtown. The radio playing in the diner interrupted programming to announce that a plane had hit one of the two World Trade Center towers. We thought it was a private pilot from New Jersey flying too close to the building.

A few minutes later the radio announced that another American Airlines 727 had piled into the second tower. America was under attack. We rushed back to our room and watched TV in horror at what had happened and was happening. Terry nearly fainted and broke into tears as the first tower came down. She wanted to go to St. Thomas Episcopal Church on Fifth Avenue.

Others had the same idea. Service was already in session when we arrived. After a few moments of meditation we went back to Fifth Avenue and noticed hundreds of people walking north. They all looked shell shocked and some were covered in ash.

The basement of the church opened and out came a group of four and five-year-old kindergartners all tied together with a rope. The teacher was oblivious to what had just happened.

It took us awhile to realize we were now trapped in Manhattan. No cars, buses, subways, trains or planes could get in or out. Police sirens were everywhere as rumors flew. Would the cultural center of the nation be hit next? Lincoln Center?

We then found out the Pentagon was also hit and another airliner crashed in Pennsylvania.

Terry and I were among the throngs of people flocking to corner convenience stores to quickly find some food. No telling how long we would be stranded in the city. We hurriedly purchased dumb things (which we never used) like canned beans and Franco-American spaghetti.

We went to bed that night scared to death. In the morning we were happily surprised when we found out our favorite restaurant, Café des Artistes, would be open for the week. They had just received their weekly supplies the prior morning.

We didn't want to go near the crash site so spent our time walking through parts of Central Park we had never seen before. An especially touching moment occurred when we came onto a small courtyard where a man was playing his guitar with a string missing. He sang the saddest rendition of the *Star-Spangled Banner*. We both cried.

Not knowing when air service would be back or when the trains would run, we explored the idea of buying a car and driving to Minnesota. I called my son Chris, who was thinking about buying a new van, and suggested I buy one in New York and sell it back to him. No way. He wanted to choose his own car make and model.

Luckily we were on the first Northwest flight out of LaGuardia on Friday night.

Neither of us feels quite the same about New York City. Being there now reminds us of that horrible event.

SOME BAD DAYS

Dear Cork

OCTOBER 2007. WE WERE ALL AT THE RIVER closing the cabin for the winter. A fun event with the whole family. I was driving the truck down toward the cabin, slowing down because the kids were using blowers to blow the leaves off the driveway. Removing the leaves from the tarmac prevents a lot of slipping and sliding in the spring. I was moving at a slow crawl when Terry came running toward me screaming at the top of her lungs to stop. Daughter Molly was screaming too.

Cork, our beloved Wheaton Terrier, must have thought that I was slowing down to let him in the truck and got caught under the front tire. I didn't know whether to back up or go forward. I panicked. Everyone was now screaming. Son-in-law Kurt made sure the little kids backed away so they would not see poor Cork.

We didn't know where the closest pet hospital was. Terry held Cork in her arms as Molly drove my car in search of a pet hospital. She found one in Blaine which was in the opposite direction I was heading.

I did a high-speed turn around on the highway.

I drove at least 25 miles over the speed limit, sobbing out of control. I could not stop crying. When I reached the hospital, Molly sent me in to see the vets and Terry. I saw poor Terry bent over Cork's face, giving him kisses. The vets told us how severely damaged he was. He couldn't make urine, there was no hope.

Cork's eyes were open and as beautiful as ever. We watched the injection and kissed Cork one last time as his eyes closed.

I went out to the truck and cried as loudly and as long as I ever had in my life. I could not believe what I had done to our wonderful puppy.

Terry and I agreed that we would never have another dog. It's just too painful.

About a year later Terry found a litter of Wheatons in Baltimore that were descendants of Cork's grandfather. Frozen sperm worked its magic.

Soon Terry got off a Delta flight in Minneapolis carrying a small dog case with a 12-week-old reddish-brown puppy. We called him Cash. His registered name was Rock of Cashel, a well-known place in Ireland. Wheaton Terriers are an Irish breed.

Cash had an almost perfect life for nearly twelve years. Unrestrained in our neighbor's and our backyards in town and free to roam over ten acres at the cabin on the St. Croix River. He was a very happy dog. He went everywhere with us.

At his last annual checkup, the vet discovered a cancerous growth in Cash's jaw. Terry and I made the difficult decision to put Cash down before the growth began to cause him pain.

On the day of Cash's trip to doggy heaven I fried some bacon for him. I let him eat the bacon out of the pan once it cooled, grease and all.

It was a chilly day in October. I took Cash for a ride in my convertible with the top down. He loved to sit tall and stick his head up in the wind. I passed a McDonald's on my way to daughter Kate's house. We were going to let Cash play with Kate's dog, Melby, one last time. "Cash, would you like a Big Mac?" He woofed it down and played with Melby for a while. On the way home, we passed the golden arches again.

He seemed to recognize them. "How about some chicken McNuggets, Cash?" I bet he thought he had died and gone to heaven.

An hour later he gently died and did go to doggy heaven.

Terry said, "No more dogs." But then again…

Our dog, Cork. *Cash was a wonderful dog.*

Governor Carlson

ARNE CARLSON

Win, Lose, Win

I GREW TIRED OF LIVING AT THE CHI PSI FRATERNITY during the winter of my senior year. The graduate student house counselor, Arne Carlson, a Chi Psi from Williams College, was also tired of communal living so we decided to rent an apartment for the spring and summer quarters. Our apartment was in a dull three-story dark brick building at 800 University Avenue in Minneapolis.

We hardly saw each other during the quarter. I was working almost full time at the *Star Tribune* and debating on various campuses around the country. Arne was in grad school and in an academic as well as romantic struggle. He was dating Barbara Duffy, a soon to be famous and controversial Minnesota broadcaster and author. They were soon married.

Arne was a Democrat when I left for the Army in 1960 and was a Republican when I returned two and a half years later. When I asked him what happened he replied he wanted to pursue a career in politics.

The Democratic Party was crowded with great potential candidates for the next several decades. There was more opportunity for him in the Republican Party. So Arne became a liberal Republican in a normally conservative party.

I co-founded Carmichael Lynch in 1962. Arne ran for Minneapolis City Council in 1964 against Richard Fransen. He wanted me to handle his advertising, pro bono of course. My greatest contribution was a direct mailer which simulated the official tax form which was about to arrive in the mail. The envelope looked like the real thing. When you opened it the tax form was screened back to grey. A large red stamp across the body of the statement said, "Richard Fransen pledged to not raise taxes. Yet he flew home to break a tie in the Council which resulted in higher taxes."

We held a glorious victory celebration which was dampened quickly by a Minnesota Supreme Court ruling that nullified the election. The tax form deception, as the Supreme Court called it, could confuse the elderly. It caused Arne (the winner) to lose the election. I was crestfallen and embarrassed. All the work in the campaign was useless because of my mailer. However, Richard Fransen failed to file with the courts within 24 hours after the ruling. Arne was again declared the victor.

Twenty years later after serving on the Minneapolis City Council, as a Senator in the State Legislature and as State Auditor, Arne became a two-term Governor of the state of Minnesota. In 2017 Arne received a letter from the judge who issued the tax mailer ruling. He apologized and said he had needed an example to scare off future misleading messages.

Joan and Fritz played parts in my St. Croix summer pageant.

WALTER MONDALE

What A Nice Guy

I HAVE KNOWN WALTER F. MONDALE since the late 1960s when he was a first-term US Senator. His two top staffers at that time were looking for a good Democrat to do media placement and creative for his upcoming election. Fritz and his staff took a liking to me.

Fritz made me proud when he was the featured speaker at a large housing conference for suppliers, builders and public officials. About a thousand people were in attendance. Little did I know that the homebuilder's association made much more of me than I really was. Fritz gave me and Carmichael Lynch a big shout out.

On another occasion, I was having dinner with my parents celebrating their anniversary at the Northstar Inn in downtown Minneapolis. Fritz came across the room and flattered me in front of Mom and Dad. His acknowledgment made me look successful at a time when "successful" would not have been a good description of my business.

Over the years I would see the former Vice President at political fundraisers. He was always friendly. It wasn't until he became Ambassador to Japan that I had more substantive discussions with him. It helped that I could speak more Japanese than he could.

I enjoyed a few strolls around Lake of the Isles with Fritz always talking politics. We discussed the St. Croix River on our walk one day and he asked me to alert him if I ever heard of a place on the river coming up for sale.

Within the month, Ellie and Jim Wittenberg told me they would be selling their place. I called Fritz. He immediately drove up and bought the place. Both seller and buyer sent me a bottle of fine champagne as a commission.

I would see him often at the hardware store in Scandia and each year he came to the Copas tennis tournament dinner. He good-naturedly agreed to perform in the big pageant I produced in 2006. He also loved a parody I wrote of *The Sound of Music* which was performed on John Holman's deck in 2008. I called it *The Sound of the River.*

He was wonderful person. He loved the St. Croix River and was a guiding force in the river's designation as a National Scenic Riverway. Fritz was proud of the Carter-Mondale administration. No one ever did anything to embarrass them during their tenure. I can't think of any other administration that can make that claim other than Obama's. When I asked him to sum up his four years in the administration, he replied, "We told the truth, obeyed the law and kept the peace."

A final ironic note. Terry served in the Carter-Mondale administration.

GRAVES VS. BACHMANN

If You Win You Lose

My friend and partner in the Loews Hotel, Jim Graves, was so upset with Congresswoman Michele Bachmann he decided to run against her in Minnesota's sixth congressional district. Jim was originally from St. Cloud and was well known in the area.

Jim did not expect to win and only a few of us knew he only wanted to scare her enough so she wouldn't run again. Jim became alarmed when he realized he actually might win. As a fierce competitor he wanted to win but as a rational businessman he didn't want to win. Being a first-term congressman in the minority party was not his idea of a great way to spend his time and money...and money was an all-important factor.

The national Democratic Party did not think Jim had a chance and did very little to help. They recommended some staff personnel who were, at the very least, dead on arrival. The campaign manager from Mississippi was stuck for an answer if you asked him, "How's it going?"

Jim switched gears. He asked his son Adam, a philosophy professor at the University of Denver, to take time off and run the campaign. We replaced the deadly dull finance professional with Jim's sons Ben and Adam and his brother John Graves. I became Jim's steering committee.

As with everything in his life, Jim gave it his all and, shazam, he started to show a steady rise in the polls. Finally, we had enough traction to start raising money...other than the $350,000 Jim lent the campaign.

Garrison Keillor, the radio celebrity, gave us a big boost by hosting two fundraisers. One at his home and the other at his bar in Lake Wobegon. We chartered a bus to the bar. I composed a song to the tune of *Bye Bye Birdie* (Bachmann) and taught it to everyone on the bus. When we arrived at the bar we were greeted by a crowd twice as large as expected. The song, Garrison and Jim were big hits.

Jim was careful not to talk about Michele's weirdness during the campaign. Everyone already knew about it. She was weird and ineffective. After three terms in the House she could only claim one success, a controversial bridge over the St. Croix River. Even then it took a congressman from the Wisconsin side and two US senators from Minnesota and Wisconsin to make it happen

(Michele went on to run for President of the United States as the sweetheart of the Tea Party. She won her first primary in Iowa.)

In the last few weeks of Jim's campaign, the Democratic National Committee threw in $250K and some big names to help at fundraisers.

Congressman Barney Frank from NY came out to help. He drew a big crowd at a high-ticket price. Barney was openly gay. Michelle thought her chances might improve if her staff could get photos and videos of Jim and Barney standing together. Barney was savvy and never got close to Jim until the end of the party.

Jim, Barney and I got on an elevator to go downstairs and have dinner. As we got on, Michele's videographer stepped on with us hoping to get some intimate footage. Just before the door closed, Jim stepped off, leaving the three of us on the ride down.

Barney looked at the video guy and said to him, "Your boss and I have something in common." "What could that possibly be?" he replied.

Barney said, "We are both married to gay men." It was rumored that Michele's husband was in the closet even though his business was counseling gays to go straight. "Pray the Gay Away" was the battle cry of the religious right.

With two weeks to go we had lots of money and asked the party media pros for advice about what to do. "Just run the same TV commercials over and over again," they said as they charged Jim a 15% commission for doing nothing.

We took great joy in firing them and taking on the media task ourselves. I found myself 50 years later doing what I did way back when... writing, producing and buying media for a client. I hired a local media firm at 5%, cancelled TV and bought all radio. On radio Jim's message could be pinpointed in the district versus wasting money on regional TV.

We were running a poll just as my best commercial went on air. That single commercial moved the needle substantially in Jim's favor.

One of our neighbors provided the voice-over with a local accent. The commercial started talking about Michele's passion for protecting the unborn. A listener would think it was going to be pro-Michele. But the commercial went on to cite the Children's Defense Fund's rating of Michele as fifth from the bottom in Congress for voting against legislation to help children in the areas of health, nutrition and education. The commercial almost pushed Jim over the top, and would have forced him to start fundraising immediately for the next campaign in only two years.

Jim and I saw firsthand the influence of money in campaigns and hated it.

Jim only wanted to scare Michele so she wouldn't run next time. Instead, he scared himself...by almost winning. He did scare her. She announced quietly at midnight she would not run again.

BORING COMMENCEMENT SPEECH?

Not With Katharine Hepburn

DAUGHTER MOLLY GRADUATED from Bryn Mawr College, a women's school near Philadelphia. The graduation ceremony was held in the middle of the beautiful campus on a lovely spring day.

I was not looking forward to the graduation commencement address. They are always the same, with bland advice and tired slogans... One step at a time, but always forward...."

When I learned the commencement speaker was Bryn Mawr alum, Katharine Hepburn, I changed my mind. I was looking forward to it.

She was eighty, beautiful and had a pronounced tremor in her voice and hands. She had Parkinson's disease yet she delivered a forceful and dramatic address about the women's movement and the responsibilities of this graduating class.

At the end of the speech, she moved to the side of the podium and went to the edge of the stage. Her closing remarks: "Young women, go out in the world and be prepared to be knocked down." She dramatically bent way over and placed her trembling hands, palms down inches from the floor. She then threw her hands up over her head and said, "But you must rise up and be prepared to be knocked down again."

Her hands went down again, close to the floor. In the bent-over position, she looked out at the graduates, placed her finger over her lips and said, "But do not get knocked up." She held the position and said, to a stunned audience, "Yes I said it. You and only you, are in charge of your body. Thank you very much."

The greatest shock was when David Bennett (in the white shirt) announced he would not be able to attend next year. He had terminal cancer.

BOYS' NIGHT OUT

They Never Grew Up

In the early to mid-'90s, Jim Zavoral and I invited a group of 14 to 18 tennis players to the St. Croix River for an afternoon of tennis, cocktails, swimming, dinner, wine and stories. A tradition had begun.

In the beginning the dinner conversation focused on telling the best jokes of the year. As time went on and everyone aged, the stories became more personal. We often told stories about the misbehavior of some of the guests from previous years.

Everyone slept over either in our cabins or in nearby river cabins so that no one would drive long distances while over the legal limit. A few were not able to control their intake and reacted in strange ways.

Dr. Bob Nelson liked to drink but could only handle two drinks. He always had three and would then disappear. He would either walk home or try to drive. After the first two years, I took away his car keys to prevent him from driving. In later years, I blocked the driveway with my truck, thwarting those clever ones who brought two sets of keys.

Ashley Haase, a regent's professor at the U of M, would always give us an update on his AIDS research. Ashley had predicted the AIDS epidemic with no cure or prevention in sight at that time. In 2010 he gave the most promising report of all those years. There was a possible cure on the horizon. Ashley over imbibed one year and got lost in the woods. A search party found him sleeping down by the creek.

Mike Murphy scared us when we couldn't find him. We searched everywhere. We were about to call the sheriff's office when I once again searched the little cabin and found him wedged between the mattress and the wall, sound asleep.

We always took bets on whose wife would be the first to call. Jim Johnson was the only one who called his wife and asked to be picked up and driven home.

John Gabbert told us his father was going to end his suffering from Lou Gehrig's disease. A week later we read about his suicide in the paper.

Gary Olin told the sad story of his daughter being involved in a fatal pedestrian accident while her weird boyfriend was driving. He disappeared and she was charged with vehicular homicide. She hung herself in the jail cell.

This was a well-read and informed group and enjoyed heated political debates. Bruce Thomson, a Republican, always found himself outnumbered 14 to 3. One of the highlights of the evening was predicting the next year's major events – what would the Dow Jones be, what baseball and football standings would be, and above all political predictions. These would be recorded and read to the group the following year.

Dick Caldecott, retired dean of the School of Chemistry, was always the oldest and one of the best tennis players. Dick was 85 in 2010. The event was always the highlight of his year.

As age started to wear out our joints, more and more started to play golf. In 2011 we invited Jack Supple, Joe Selvaggio and Jim Graves to join our golf group.

Terry's rule was the cabin had to be clean before she would appear the next day. We always made quite a mess. Eighteen drinking, storytelling men, trying to clean up at midnight after a banquet of salmon, fresh corn, black beans with green sauce, fresh tomatoes with basil and mozzarella cheese and pie with ice cream for dessert. Doing the dishes and putting them away while under the influence was chaotic. Sometimes it would take most of the summer to find where certain pots and bowls had been hidden. They were in most unusual places like dishware in the oven.

We finally aged out and held the final night in 2014.

Las Palomas, our home in the Land of Enchantment. We used it 70 plus days a year for 22 years.

LAS PALOMAS

Home In Sante Fe

Terry and I took a belated honeymoon trip in March 1983. We skied in Steamboat Springs and then headed to Santa Fe, New Mexico, one of Terry's favorite spots. It was my first trip to the land of enchantment. I was taken with its beauty and the convergence of the three ethnic groups that live in the state.

We began to return annually and started looking for a place to rent long term or perhaps buy. One Sunday, during brunch at Rancho Encantado, Terry found an ad for a house for sale in the local paper that sounded interesting and was just up the road from the ranch. We decided to drive up and look at it.

Two cars, one a realtor's, were in the drive. We knocked and walked in. Terry knew immediately that this was her house. She knew without touring the home in its entirety. The realtor was talking to a woman and as he turned to greet us he exclaimed, "Lee Lynch." I said, "Mike Baker." Mike was a friend of mine from Big Sky, Montana and a red-hot realtor in the area.

He could tell we were interested in the house. We decided to leave before we further piqued the interest of the other prospective buyer.

Antoine Predock, a famous southwestern architect, had designed the house. (He later became internationally famous and designed the Alumni Center at the University of Minnesota.)

There was a savings and loan crisis at the time and Mike told us the S&L with the mortgage was likely to go under. A federal government program to clean up the entire real estate mess had placed the loan with a special servicer. Mike thought the S&L might accept an offer in the amount of the unpaid balance, $369,000, to clean up their portfolio fast.

Terry wanted to offer more but $369,000 was a stretch for us at that time. We made the offer without a lot of optimism that it would be accepted.

We were going through a ton of mail after a planned vacation in Antigua. Terry was crestfallen when she saw the house, her house, on the cover of *Architecture*. She was about to go into a total depression when my assistant Rosanne called and congratulated us on our new home.

We were stunned. They had accepted our offer. The following day Hall Wendel, a client and friend, called to ask us about Santa Fe. He had seen a house on the cover of *Architecture* and wanted to check it out. He was amazed to learn we were its new owners.

Shortly after we received an offer to buy the house for $500,000. The cover story and Predock's mounting fame had an immediate impact. We were able to get a mortgage in the full amount because of its perceived value.

We named it Las Palomas, the Doves. We finished the courtyard and decided to build a guesthouse a few years later. We turned to the now-famous Predock to see if he would design a guesthouse. A staff member, not Predock, returned the call. He said the firm would do the job for 20% of the project cost plus $150 per hour of design time and supervision. It was a polite way to say no. They no longer did any small projects.

Terry asked our dear friend and architect Peter Kramer to go to Santa Fe and come up with an idea for the guesthouse. Peter did not turn to other houses in the area for inspiration. Instead he went to the local Indian pueblos in search of an idea.

Peter proposed a building which simulated an Indian holy place, a kiva. It was circular and had a stairway to the roof that bisected the structure. Over the rooftop skylight, he designed a complex but fun system of mirrors which during the summer and winter solstice would capture the sun and direct a shaft of light to a prism in the hole of the floor, illuminating the whole room on only those two dates. He got the idea from Anasazi kivas. It was brilliant but far too complicated for us to pull off.

We used the home for about 70 days a year for 22 years. We loved it. When we both retired we decided to sell it so we had more flexibility in our lives. We sold at the top of the market to friends Fred and Marie-Noëlle Meyer.

They invited us to stay in the house after they bought it and all its furnishings but it felt too weird. We did it once but never again.

We miss Las Palomas and visit Santa Fe frequently.

Central Park in NYC.

A surprise processi in the deep woods of northern Swede at 11 p.m.

Yo Yo Ma likes Lee's joke.

MUSICAL HIGHLIGHTS

Four Stand Out

I'M CERTAIN EVERYONE HAS MEMORIES of his or her favorite concerts. Only four really stand out for me. Odd given the business I was in and my wife Terry's love of classical music and opera. You would think more than just a couple would be memorable.

NUMBER ONE

Simon and Garfunkel's reunion concert at Central Park in New York City was one. It was a warm May evening. Over 500,000 people sat on the ground, picnicked, smoked cigarettes and grass. The smell of grass was heavy in the air. Terry and I bought some prosciutto and cheese at a deli and sat on a blanket for hours. We could not even see the stage, but it was still a memorable event. Was it possible our budding courtship was the reason and not the music?

NUMBER TWO

Yo-Yo Ma, Bobby McFerrin and Hugh Wolff performed for almost two hours at Dr. Fallon's home on Lake of the Isles. It was the most intimate and exclusive musical event I have ever experienced. We were invited to the evening because Terry was chair of the St. Paul Chamber Orchestra board at that time. There was seating for only 40 in Dr. Fallon's music room. Terry and I were seated in the front row almost touching Yo-Yo.

After the performance, I had a long conversation with Yo-Yo and failed to take him up on his request to visit Carmichael Lynch the next day because I had to travel. Too bad. He was a great guy and extremely interested in advertising.

NUMBER THREE

The Lion King was built in Minneapolis and ran for 12 weeks before it moved on to Broadway. Terry and I attended the dress rehearsal with a few others from the Disney organization and theater staff. When the African witch doctor entered from the corner of the stage and started to sing *Circle of Life*, we were both in awe. The stagecraft was amazing with the sun rising over the Serengeti as the music was building.

We noticed a disturbance as something started moving down the aisles behind us. As we turned a large, life-size elephant took shape, then a giraffe, then birds and cheetahs and many other animals found in Africa. They paraded slowly down the two side aisles. We looked up and saw beautiful birds circling above. All these creatures were the genius of Julie Taymor. The music continued to build as they all climbed on stage, Terry and I wept. It was a grand event.

NUMBER FOUR

It was summer solstice in Sweden. Bob and Christina Persson wanted to treat us to an authentic old-fashioned Swedish solstice party. They drove us to their grandfather's hunting cabin at the top of a remote farm in northern Sweden. A tiny old log building with low ceilings all dark and smoky reminded us of our cabin on the St. Croix. About 10 p.m. their brothers, sisters, cousins, nieces and nephews joined us in making a Swedish solstice cross covered with vines and wildflowers. It was about ten feet tall with long colorful ribbons attached at the top. When the cross was finished and raised, everyone had a beer, ate smoked meats and freshly caught grilled fish. I thought the party was almost over.

It had just begun. We could hear music in the distance. A violin. An accordion. Then out of the midnight mist came a Swedish band in full native dress. It was beautiful.

We sang and danced around the maypole, drank beer, sang more songs and kept the festivities going until the midnight sun started to come up in the east. A solstice to remember.

The official Reykjavik Athletic Club patch.

REYKJAVIK

The Icelandic Attorney

AROUND 1968 I STARTED TO LOOK FOR A WAY to own a summer vacation place. My problem was I had no money.

My client and friends at Pemtom, a major real estate developer, suggested that if I could find an old resort for sale we could collectively put together an association to purchase it. That would be a way for me to be an equal owner without having to put too much money upfront (and a way to obscure my weak net worth and income).

I started to look in northern Minnesota and came up empty-handed. I turned to Wisconsin and discovered that the asking price for a place three or more hours from the Twin Cities was considerably less.

My criteria for a location were being next to water and easy access to a ski slope. I began looking in the Telemark, Wisconsin area. Many lakes, a modest ski hill (very modest, 600 ft. elevation) with a lodge, meeting center and dynamic owner, Tony Wise.

After looking at several places, I found an ideal spot on the Garden

Lake section of Lake Namakagon. It was on a small peninsula with an owner's home and three cabins. The others liked it and we could buy it for $50,000 cash. I could barely come up with my $12,500 but because I put the deal together, I could have the owner's home for no additional money.

Bruce Thomson built a new home on one lot. Larry Laukka tore down an old cabin and put up an experimental glued together home. Bob Davidson got the other small cabin that wasn't winterized. Bob is of Icelandic origins and named it Reykjavik without our knowledge.

For over twelve years we raised our children there. The men shared rides back and forth to the Twin Cities during the week to go to work. The Reykjavik Athletic Club built a tennis court and hired a very strange caretaker, Gill. Gilly, as we called him, was fine sober but a problem drunk. He would fall asleep at the strangest times.

I went to Reykjavik almost every other weekend year-round. My work schedule was crazy and this was a good way to keep in touch with the kids. They all liked to ski, swim and play tennis so it was a great place for them to grow up.

As time went on, Telemark underwent major expansions including a big lodge, meeting center and 60-room hotel. Lots were also sold on the new golf course. Larry was involved in building the lodge and hotel rooms and I assisted with marketing and advertising. I quit as soon as I could because I found doing business on weekends ruined my vacation experience.

Tony Wise made Telemark work by creating one of the nation's major cross-country ski centers, sponsoring a race called the Birkebeiner that drew entrants from around the US and several foreign countries.

I will never forget son Chris's training for the race undone by a sleepy father. On the big day of the race I got up a bit too late and had to rush Chris, age 13, to the starting line. What I didn't plan on was a traffic jam at the resort and having to park a mile from the start. We ran from the car to the beginning line only to hear the cannon go off and watch hundreds of skiers going up the big hill at the start. Chris broke down in tears and didn't talk to me for a week. I felt terrible.

We canoed on the Namakagon, hiked in the forest and frequently visited

Madeline Island, only an hour away. We had many happy times there.

As my marriage went downhill, I knew divorce was coming. I told the group we would be selling our cabin and be the first to leave. Everyone was truly sad, especially the other children because my skits, plays and silliness were always a hit.

I sold for $50,000. Bruce eventually bought out my buyer and Larry Laukka. His glue house had become unglued and was torn down. Bob kept his cabin even though he built a great home on Madeline Island.

On July 4, 2018, Beth Laukka, Larry's daughter, shared some recollections of Reykjavik –

"I remember the greased watermelon relay race, cherry seed spitting contests on the shuffleboard court, gunnysack races, bonfire stories and Gill preparing all day for a pig roast. And Mr. Lynch's bear hunts and his convincing act laying an egg after eating too much chicken."

Lee telling Bill Clinton a joke, not too successfully.

About a year after this picture was taken Mr. Obama ran for President.

FAMOUS NAMES

And Some Not So Famous

I NEVER THOUGHT OF MYSELF AS A GROUPIE and never took advantage of my connection to the theater business to meet the many stars we booked. However I did ask for, and got, a hug from Julie Andrews.

As a Minnesota businessperson, I knew most of the Minnesota Democratic Senators and candidates for President of the United States. Humphrey, McCarthy and Mondale. I considered Fritz a friend.

I shook hands with Michael Dukakis and Jimmy Carter, spent a little time with John Kerry and Al Gore but had the great pleasure of spending time in small meeting environments with Bill Clinton, Hillary Clinton and Barack Obama.

Terry and I met Barack Obama at Ruth Usem's home before he was a presidential candidate. There were about twenty of us at the luncheon and we were instantly impressed with Mr. Obama's style and substance. The things we liked most about him were his thoughtful answers and wisdom to say he didn't know an answer or was not up on an issue.

Bill Clinton met with about ten of us early on in his campaign when it looked like he didn't stand a chance of getting the nomination. He was a country boy governor from Arkansas. Within ten minutes we all knew he was the man. After about an hour and a half covering virtually any and all subjects, I realized he was brilliant. When I left the meeting with Ken Dayton we agreed he was our candidate.

Some top names on tour for the theaters would add a clause for a first-class golf outing in their contract. On separate occasions I took Mikhail Baryshnikov and Willie Nelson golfing at Minikahda. I had a drink with Mikhail in the clubhouse. The women in the bar were savvy enough to leave him alone. When he left they all came up to me asking if he was the famous dancer.

Willie just wanted to play. He wasn't very good. When he tucked his ponytail under his hat and put on large sunglasses you couldn't tell my golf partner was a famous entertainer. He didn't talk much and swore a lot when he missed a shot—which was quite often.

I played golf with Gene Hackman at the Boulders Resort in Arizona. He was a fun partner and appreciated me not talking about his or anyone's movies. Several years later Gene became our neighbor in Santa Fe.

My most unusual meeting was with Bishop Tutu of South Africa. Terry was named an outstanding alumni of Claremont Graduate School and Tutu was giving the address. Terry had to attend a meeting about the award ceremony and asked that I wait in the garden for her so we would go together to meet the Bishop.

I was sitting alone for a few minutes and saw the Bishop walk into the garden looking for the president of the college. Tutu, a half-hour early, was more than happy to engage me with stories about South African politics. Thank goodness I was up to speed on issues in his country. He was very curious about Minnesota so I saturated him with information.

Sarah Weddington was the attorney who argued the Roe v. Wade case and a good friend of Terry's. She soon became one of mine. Sarah stayed at our home and cabin on many occasions.

Garrison Keillor was the biggest local name I met. He did a half-hour gig at my retirement party and sang a duet with me on the Pantages stage. That led me to sing again with him on stage in his *Prairie Home Companion* radio show. Friends from around the country called to tell me I was not bad. Later I invested in his movie and was able to hug Meryl Streep and Lily Tomlin.

When Terry and I took the train from Beijing to Moscow there was a well-known military man on board, General William Westmoreland, the architect of the Vietnam debacle. I knew that if I played my cards right I could ask him a few questions he usually ducked. There were only 93 people on the train for 11 days. I knew the right occasion would occur.

I introduced myself while we were both in the club car waiting for our wives. He looked warily at my longish hair, beard and funny glasses and asked if I had served my country. Bingo. Yes sir, Sgt. E-5 Lee Lynch. He relaxed. Because my rank was Sgt. he assumed I was a volunteer, not a draftee, and could be trusted.

Over the next few days Terry and I played bridge with him and his wife and had a drink together. He was pleasant to us but not many others. The General was the highest-ranking American officer to ever go to Mongolia and he was celebrated with an amazing close order drill by the Mongolia army. They had a lot of time to practice because they'd had no war for sixty years and no imminent enemy. It was a sight to behold.

Later that day the General invited me to join him for a drink. I decided to ask my questions. My first question was when did he receive a clearly articulated mission for Vietnam. He froze and said that there never was one. Then he wanted to talk about his last job in the Army as the superintendent of West Point. I let him go on for a bit until I asked him what I knew would be my final question. I asked him what he thought of Colonel John Vann's story in *A Bright Shining Lie*. The book revealed how the US public was fooled by constant reports of battle success as measured by enemy body count. Vann suggested Westmoreland was responsible for the PR scam.

The General turned cold and told me that John Vann was a good soldier but not a good American. Then he turned away and left. He didn't speak to me for the rest of the trip.

We have had a few big names at Democratic fundraisers in our home.

Senate Majority leader Harry Reid and his wife used our home for a fundraiser and later took us to dinner at the Minikahda Club. Reid and Rahm Emanuel were supporters of our good friend Senator Amy Klobuchar. Over the years, nearly every Democrat running for Congress, mayor or governor asked us to host a fundraiser. I think we averaged four a year. Steny Hoyer, Barney Frank and several others have been our guests.

During the Obama race we held several fundraisers for various candidates. In March of 2010 we hosted an event for the National Senate Finance Campaign Committee. Both Minnesota Senators Klobuchar and Franken were at our home as well as Senator Debbie Stabenow of Michigan.

The biggest event was in 2012 with President Bill Clinton. He sat in our living room answering questions for 90 minutes with a small group of twenty people. He was, as usual, running late. As he left the house there were 50 or so people lined up on the street. All the secret service cars were a tip-off. President Clinton could not resist going down the line, posing in selfies and signing autographs for the kids. He was extremely late for a big event at the University of Minnesota honoring Walter Mondale. Fritz later blamed me for the delay.

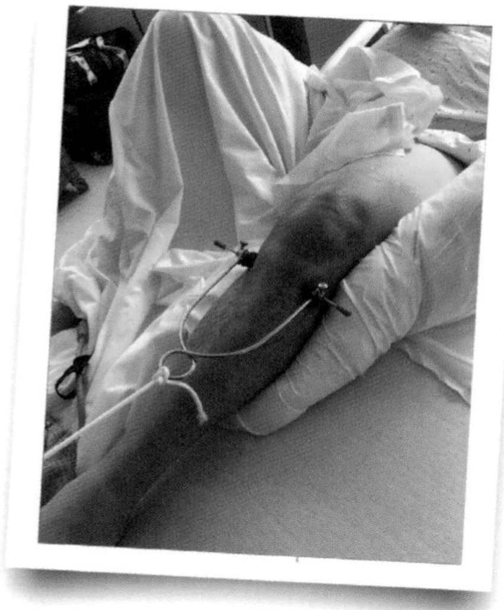

I was awake when they drilled a hole all the way through my leg.

MY BODY IS A TEMPLE

But The Temple Is Crumbling

I STARTED WRITING THIS TEN DAYS BEFORE my seventy-seventh natal day. It was during a trip to Cuba I realized I was reaching a major threshold in my life.

The first day in Cuba was scheduled to be an easy to moderate three-hour hike in the mountains near Santiago de Cuba, near where the Fidelistas launched the revolution. The hike was anything but moderate. It was five hours of climbing, tripping, sliding, and wading through four rivers. Knee-high rushing water covering large stones.

Our group was not up to such a demanding hike. I doubt the travel planners had scouted the route beforehand and a local told them it was easy. One in our group was injured and one had to be carried out by a donkey the guide summoned from a nearby village. I waded the rivers with my shoes on and threw the shoes back to the other side so others didn't have to get wet. Some said my shoes were hard to fill. Terry made three of the rivers but opted to go by horse over the last one.

One poor guy (not really poor, he was a hedge fund manager) fell while crossing ruining his camera and cell phone as well as cutting his head. He was only two steps from the shore when he stepped in a hole.

The following day was yet another trek which only a few of the younger and fittest joined. My mistake was joining the group and realizing too late I couldn't duck walk while inside a cave. Someone behind me told me to hurry up. They thought I was looking for bats or stalactites. It was the first time I could not lead the pack…it was the first time I held others up. My legs were burning and I was out of breath. I'm old.

It's funny as you age you start to think about the end game. The last suit you'll buy, the last car, the last time you'll be able to make love. Ouch, I'm not ready for this.

I was now determined to lose 20 pounds and break a sweat at least four times a week. My spinning class insured I would break a sweat. I was the oldest in the class by 20 years. I quit spinning because the small bike seat hurt my butt. I now realize my leg strength and wind won't return to my 50's or 60's standard.

I've been lucky over the years to have good health. Two hip implants, a scary recurring staph infection and a torn rotator cuff. A 52 resting heartbeat and 120/70 blood pressure. However, in the summer of 2016 I felt a weakness for about three weeks I could not explain. On the 4th of July I asked Terry to take me to the hospital, something was going on. I was diagnosed with AFib, a heart condition of an irregular beat which can be quite debilitating. While in the hospital the docs determined I also had PMR, polymyalgia rheumatica, an inflammation of muscles. I was told it was unrelated to AFib (I found that hard to believe). They put me on a heavy steroid to relieve the pain in my legs. The PMR was a misdiagnosis. It took a year for me to taper off the steroid because of the strength of the original prescription.

This October I needed a cortisone shot in my ankle for arthritis and now have a daily exercise routine for a painful right leg. I take four drugs. Flomax for the bladder, Xarelto as a blood thinner for the AFib, a daily antibiotic, Bactrim, for the staph infection and Lipitor for cholesterol.

As of this writing, I've just celebrated my 84th birthday.

I guess I'll make it to 85 in reasonable health. Then, I'm told, many other things will start to fall apart.

On February 14, 2018, I tried to hang glide without the glider. I was rushing down the stairs at home to watch Lindsey Vonn in the Olympic giant slalom on TV. She skied out and didn't finish. Neither did I. I tripped over the last three steps and fell dead weight on my right side.

Bad break. Very bad break of the body's largest bone, the femur. The surgeon told me that on a ten-point scale of bad breaks, I was a 9.5. Six months in a wheelchair, no weight on my left leg and no walking until August. While in the wheelchair I passed a kidney stone and got shingles.

The question is, what will get me, old age or Covid-19?

This is the last time I'll write about my health.

Joe's ashes and his kids flew off the river bridge.

Chet Huntley

UNUSUAL FUNERALS

And Last Moments

After my brother Tommy died in 2006, I found an interesting collection of his. He saved and filed by date prayer cards for every funeral he attended. His collection caused me to think about my most memorable funerals.

BUD THE STUD

Bud Engstrom was tall, had blond wavy hair, a military bearing and was very rich. He drove a new Thunderbird convertible while in college. He also dated the homecoming queen, the saucy Becky Nelson. I hitchhiked to work every day at the *Star and Tribune* and wished I had any kind of car, even an old clunker. Bud and I were both in the same fraternity, Chi Psi. Bud (we all called him Budly) smoked a pipe, skipped classes and regaled us with his tales of conquest with the ladies on campus.

Bud's father owned large tracks of timber in northern Minnesota and Canada. Bud joined his father's business, married Becky and prospered in Minnesota even though he changed wives three times.

Dick Bryer, a close friend, fraternity brother and a resident of Bud's hometown told me the story of Bud's demise. While checking out a large stand of timber in Canada he felt sick to his stomach and went over to a large pit the workers used as a toilet. Open-air, no seat. Bud vomited, passed out and fell into the pit of poop. Heart attack. Covered with feces, the loggers put him in the back of a lumber truck and rushed to the nearest hospital some three hours away. He died en route.

The funeral was unusual. Everyone knew how he died but no one mentioned it during the ceremony. Dick did recall that there was quite a buzz before and after. The memorable visual from the funeral was his three former wives sitting in the front row, side by side, dressed in black with black veils. Sitting with them, dressed identically, was his newest girlfriend.

He was Bud the Stud.

GREG KELSEY

Son-in-law Kurt Kelsey's brother Greg died while jogging at the age of 38. He was a successful artist and husband to our friend Sally Johnson.

I didn't know Greg well but came to know him through the longest and most loving memorial service I have ever attended.

It was held in the chapel on the Macalester College campus, Greg's alma mater. The setting was in the round and well attended. People who knew Greg simply talked about him whenever the spirit moved them. I learned that in the name of art, with a few beers under their belt, Greg and a friend spray painted the white wall at Princes' studio in Chanhassen. They scrawled some artistic slam at the world of Prince.

As the afternoon wore on, more and more people shared both fun and sad memories of Greg. Then there was a long pause. I thought the service was about to end when Greg's father, Paul Kelsey, stood up and gave a brief heartwarming yet sad commentary. Another pause. Then to everyone's amazement, his mother Dot stood up and talked about her baby boy. It was lovely and heartbreaking. And when our hearts were wrenched about as much as we could stand, Greg's wonderful wife Sally stood up. It was amazing. I will never know how the family was able to summon the strength to talk. I think the service was the right catharsis for the family.

I will never forget it.

JOE CULLIGAN

Joe was in the advertising business for many years and almost went to work for me in the '80s. He was a fun guy with an energetic family. They had a place near us on the St. Croix River so we saw them frequently on summer weekends.

When Joe left the ad business he became the transitional president of the College of Visual Arts in St. Paul. The school was on hard times. Joe learned just how hard when the furnace needed repair and he paid for it himself.

Joe contracted a form of cancer that took him quickly. He did have time to plan for his final exit and did it in spades. Joe set the new standard.

A few things were said about Joe on the steps of the school and then everyone paraded three blocks down Summit Avenue to the University Club of St. Paul for a jam-packed grand party. The parade was led by a Dixieland band. The coffin was carried by his kids.

The following weekend his wife, three kids and many grandkids came to our cabin on the St. Croix and used our pontoon to go up the river to the railroad bridge to scatter Joe's ashes.

The three kids climbed on the bridge carrying an old dynamite box with Joe's ashes. They shot off a rocket and then jumped 40-feet into the river below throwing the ashes in the air.

On the way back to the city his daughter-in-law (her father is Dustin Hoffman) turned on the radio and heard a song called *Hauling Joe Down the River*...the St. Croix to New Orleans.

Wow. Tears were shed by all.

I think Terry and I saw Joe go by the next day. I called out to him... great show Joe.

CHET HUNTLEY

Chet Huntley was one of the best-known American newsmen and an anchor in the top-rated NBC *Evening News* (back when everyone watched the evening news). He retired in 1968 and lent his name to the developers of Big Sky, Montana. He was given 1% interest in the business and a beautiful home at Big Sky.

Northwest Airlines, Conoco, Montana Power and Light, and Chrysler Real Estate were the owners of Big Sky. Carmichael Lynch was hired as their first agency because of our real estate experience. I liked getting exposed to developers for possible future business opportunities.

I was summoned to Chet's office to show him the first ad we were producing. He was sitting in a swivel chair and lost his breath as he turned to face me. I thought he was going to die right there. He recovered and nodded off. He died the next day. His largest on-air client was Lucky Strike cigarettes, the most likely cause of his emphysema.

We were there with a film crew to shoot a commercial but it was delayed because of Chet's memorial service.

The service took place at 7,000 feet in front of the Huntley Lodge with Lone Mountain in the background. About forty people were seated as it began to snow–big flakes that became bigger and bigger. They were the size of ping-pong balls and not a breeze. The large flakes fell on the people gathered and our film director Maury Hurley sensed a great scene. He quickly set up a camera to film everyone covered with snow. The pastor was hatless and the snow fit him like a nun's cap, white and deep. Only his mouth and eyes could be seen.

It was a mystical event. Everything went white. The film could have been a prizewinner, but the family did not want it shown.

1969 movie poster for Downhill Racer.

HELICOPTER SKIING CAPER

A Bad Prat Fall

I HAD NEVER SKIED IN REALLY DEEP POWDER except for a few days in Big Sky so I was extremely apprehensive as the chopper lifted off from our base camp in the Selkirk Mountains of British Columbia.

My dear friend David Bennett, an experienced powder hound, Worth Bruntjen, a financial wizard with Piper Jaffray, and Gary and Suzie Rappaport were the other Minnesotans among the 27 skiers in our party.

We were divided into groups of nine based on ability. Worth and I were at the second-lowest level. Both of us should have been one level lower as we had trouble keeping up.

Our first run was exhausting since we hadn't acclimated to the altitude. As the day wore on, we began to adjust to the altitude and our skiing improved. It was still exhausting. The chopper would drop you off on a glacier at 0° and you ski down 3,000 vertical feet to temperatures of about 25°. Sweat permeated our ski clothes because of all the calories we were burning. We would get to the pickup spot wringing wet and then walk to the chopper with its blades creating a 30-mile an hour wind...cooling us off considerably. Then the ascent to the next glacier where the same wind from the blades combined with the cold would freeze everything on your body. . .gloves, faces and masks. Only when you started the descent did you begin to thaw out. It's no wonder I lost eight pounds in five days even though we ate five meals a day.

At night we stayed in a snowed-in old mining camp. . .bare bones. My room was in an old mobile home with a snow tunnel to the dining room. Everyone came in dead tired, drank a little wine and went to bed early, except for the last night.

Knowing we only had a half-day left to ski everyone was in the mood to party and we did. The chef could play the zither, so we sang and danced until an accident stopped the party.

One of the skiers had kept to himself for the whole trip. He bought a discounted trip at the last moment through a Denver broker. He was by far the best skier in the group and had been a stunt skier for the Robert Redford movie, *Downhill Racer.* He was an odd duck. That night he came out of his shell and danced on top of the table. Being under the influence, he got dizzy spinning around on the tabletop and fell off on top of a wine glass that was sitting on the floor. It was his wine glass. He landed precisely on his rectum, breaking the glass and deeply cutting his rectum and surrounding area.

Three in our party were doctors, two emergency physicians from Denver and a surgeon from California. When they examined our patient they realized that glass fragments had to be extracted from the wound and he would need several stitches. It was going to be further complicated because he had to evacuate his bowels.

The doctors were worried about the legality of the situation. None had a Canadian license and all had been drinking quite a bit. . .grounds for a juicy lawsuit. They judged me to be fairly sober (David had gone to bed or he would have been the chosen one). My job was to assist them and decide who was best able to stitch up the patient.

The doc from California had to withdraw from consideration because he had the most to drink and it showed. I had the two emergency docs draw straws to see who would do the job and get the legal exposure. We agreed we would never identify under any circumstance who did the work in case of a lawsuit. And we would not mention this to anyone in our group.

A large chair was turned over and a mattress was placed over it with a lamp and flashlight hung directly over the apex. I was busy getting hot water from the kitchen so I missed some of the prep work. When I returned with the water I took a look at our drugged fellow skier with his rear end projecting upward, the gash very visible and bleeding profusely...there was blood everywhere. I vomited and then fainted. I missed the actual sewing. I never would have to lie in court if it ever got to that.

The next day we all assembled for breakfast and then on to the launch pad for our last run. We were stunned to see the "patient" come out of his shack in a powder blue, one-piece ski suit with a hang glider strapped to his back. The guy was not only going to ski but was going to hang glide off a precipice located above the camp. When one of the docs tried to talk him out of it, they realized he was high on something, most likely cocaine.... which explained his isolation.

Our group of nine finished the downhill run first and had the opportunity to witness our patient launch above us in his blue ski suit stained bright red on both legs. He broke his stitches.

He had to be flown immediately to Calgary for an emergency procedure. His emergency took the chopper that was to evacuate us. We had to sit on our hands all day hoping we could still make our flights out of Vancouver. We didn't and had to spend the night. We couldn't get out and a new group couldn't get in.

We never inquired about his condition. Somehow, I didn't care.

LAW, ORDER AND DAVID LYKKEN

Facing The Long Blue Line

MY NEXT-DOOR NEIGHBOR at 4600 Emerson Avenue South was an unusually interesting man. David Lykken, and his wife Harriet, were hardcore anti-Vietnam war protestors and held many peace-oriented fundraisers in their home.

David was a distinguished professor of psychology at the University of Minnesota and Harriet was a talented community organizer. They were good neighbors and good friends. We also shared a driveway that ran between our homes.

One evening the Lykken's were hosting a fundraiser to plant flowers at the missile silos in North Dakota. I planned to attend the event after I went to see the movie, *Woodstock*. I arrived home to find their house surrounded by police cars and a paddy wagon.

The mayor of Minneapolis, Charles Stenvig, was a law-and-order former police officer and hated any anti-Vietnam activities. When someone tipped him off about the event at the Lykken's, he sent the full swat squad, automatic weapons and flak jackets.

They had a search warrant to enter the house and made everyone go outside to be frisked and loaded into the paddy wagon. The presumed reason for the bust was selling liquor without a license. People put 50-cents in a basket when they took a beer or soft drink and that seemed to constitute breaking the law.

I stood in my driveway and watched the police search the house. Two flashlights were evident in the basement until someone found the light switch. Another officer was closely examining the windowsill on the second floor. I went over to David who was standing at the paddy wagon with his hands on its side while the police searched him. I asked if I should call his lawyer and David replied, "The dumb shits don't realize they just arrested my attorney."

Close to thirty people were hauled downtown, fingerprinted and released on bond. I remained at the Lykken's house and noticed that the police removed a large file from their son Matthew's room. The file contained suspicious columns of numbers. The police later discovered the numbers were innocuous and part of Matt's fascination with baseball statistics. (He went on to earn a doctorate in math.)

Unfortunately for the police, they had a warrant to search only the first floor yet they searched all floors. David sued the police department and each officer individually for the illegal search. All seventeen police officers lied and said no one had been on any floor other than the first.

I took the stand in the trial facing all seventeen cops standing shoulder to shoulder. I told the judge what I observed while standing in the driveway that night. It was my word against the police. I must admit I found the situation quite intimidating. They even wore their weapons. They glared at me as I caught them in their lie. I hoped I didn't have even a parking violation for fear they would get back at me.

David, in his wisdom, did not sue the city for a lot of money. The city had to pay only his legal expenses and $5,000 for his son to buy a Volkswagen. He did however sue each officer personally for $3000 to be taken out of their pay each month for three years.

Every time I hear a reference to *Woodstock* I think of that evening.

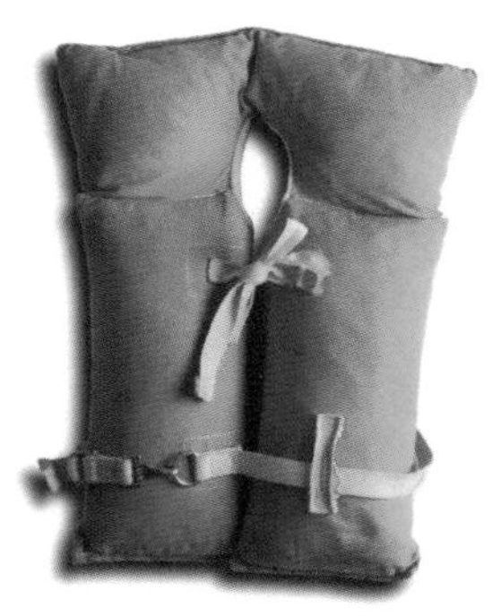

OFFICER GENE MANLY

Bane Of The St. Croix

A FEW HORROR STORIES WERE CIRCULATING in Marine on St. Croix about a DNR officer who patrolled the Upper St. Croix River. Everyone said he was weird, power-hungry and tough.

One Friday morning I was going north on my pontoon boat from the marina to our cabin when hidden in some tree branches by the side of the river was Officer Manly with a civilian buddy. He turned on his blinking lights and siren and pulled me over.

He wanted to see my license (which no one ever carries on a pontoon) and my life preserver. He noted that the jacket was not in good repair and that it did not fit. I laughed and said I would lose weight. He looked at me sternly, said my conduct was out of order and I would have to appear in court on Monday.

"For what?" I thought he was joking. "Your boat was on plane. You broke the law for speeding." "But officer, this old 20 horse off-brand motor couldn't get this boat on plane if it had a 50-mph tailwind."

"Tell that to the judge," he said as he tore the ticket off his pad and handed it to me with a glare.

"Gene, this is a joke, right?" "You do not address an officer of the state by his first name," he sternly replied and roared off.

I had to go to court in Stillwater the following Monday. Since I was early I decided to have breakfast at a nearby café.

Once in the courthouse, I was told to sit in the front row and rise when the judge came in. As I sat waiting, a police officer opened a side door and escorted in three men who had been held overnight in jail for disturbing the peace and fighting. The guy sitting next to me had his ear bitten off in the fight and was wearing a large bandage. This was weird. Then the judge arrived.

He looked to be in his late twenties or early thirties. He called my name, read the charge "boat on plane" and asked me to declare either guilty or not guilty. I said, "Your honor if you could only see the age of my boat..." "GUILTY, OR NOT GUILTY," he said loudly.

"Your honor, I have an old 20 horse motor...." "GUILTY, OR NOT GUILTY. You can plead not guilty, hire an attorney and have a trial or plead guilty and pay the $85 fine." I looked down and only then realized that the red napkin from the café was tucked under my chin. I paid.

A few years later Officer Manly stopped me again while going upriver with all the kids. He made us show him all the life preservers to prove we had one for each person. As he inspected one jacket, an old one, he gave the strap a light tug. It tore the jacket open and the stuffing fell out.

Officer Manly was now terribly upset and kept saying over and over it was not his fault. I thought he was going to cry. He was clearly unstable. Then I noticed the gun strapped to his thigh.

The following week I called a friend at the DNR. Carmichael Lynch was doing some pro bono work for him and he was quite open about Manly. He was assigned to the upper river because it was calm and free of violations and Manly was having emotional problems.

He had a gun!

My friend later called and told me that Manly had been reassigned to work at the DNR shooting range.

The uniform was a bit small.

THE PERFECT PITCH

Never Bet Against Me

I WAS SURPRISED WHEN THE MINNESOTA TWINS contacted me to say I had been selected to throw out the first pitch at the season home game on May 14, 2016, Twins vs Baltimore.

I thought a great way to raise money for a good cause might be to ask folks to bet on whether I could throw a perfect pitch, a strike. I chose Second Harvest Heartland food bank as the charity and began challenging friends to bet against me.

My proposition–if I didn't throw a strike, I would pay the waged amount to Second Harvest Heartland. If I did throw a strike, they all had to pay up. My assistant Rosanne would collect the money. We cut the betting off at $2,000. Unfortunately, it crept up to $2,250 before we stopped taking bets.

I had a plan. Most guests who throw out the first pitch can't get the ball to the plate. I would practice and try not to embarrass myself.

Neighbor Bill Bowen, three houses from us on Park Lane, has two sons who were great baseball players. I knew Bill was an old coach. Be darned if he didn't have all the equipment – gloves, balls, a real home plate and pitcher's rubber. "Beware of gravity," Bill said right away. "The ball wants to drop down, so start high. Don't worry about speed."

I practiced throwing for six days...short sessions because I wanted to save my arm. The first day I could not get the ball the regulation distance between the pitcher's mound and home base–60'6." On the following days I got better and finally could consistently get the ball to the catcher, his son Major. Bill made me use the windup pitch pitcher's use when there is a man on base because there are fewer moving body parts. I was throwing strikes about 50% of the time.

On the big day, I was escorted into the stadium, given a too small Twins uniform shirt and cap, and led on to the field. When we arrived a light rain had started and the grounds crew was covering the field with the tarp.

They offered me a chance to come back on another night but I knew it was now or never. We had to find the mound and the home plate under the tarp which caused a few bettors to claim I wasn't regulation. I didn't like pitching from a slippery tarp with no warm-up. But I let fly a medium speed perfect strike called by a legitimate umpire.

Shortly after my pitch, the whole game was called a rainout. But my perfect pitch stood. And the doubters paid up.

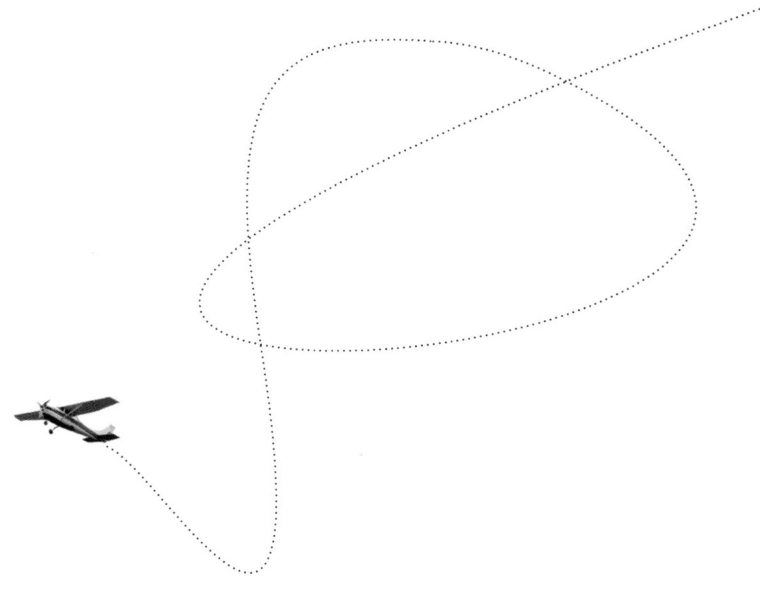

WILD BLUE YONDER

Stay Grounded

I HAVE BEEN REALLY SCARED FOUR TIMES while in an airplane.

The pilots who flew Fred and Marie-Noëlle Meyer and Terry and me to Timbuktu had never been there. We noticed as the sun was setting the pilots were consulting a Michelin road map, the same map we were using. They had no contact with the airport or ground control. (We later learned the generators in town and at the airport were down.) Night comes quickly in the desert, like turning off a light switch. The pilots faced sudden darkness with no ability to follow the roads below.

The only light we could see in the distance came from small cooking fires. Was that Timbuktu? We had no choice. We had to assume it was. We were running out of fuel. Only a sliver of the moon kept its glow as we began to circle the dark forms of the town below. We circled and circled. We had time to think about dying, especially with jerry cans of high-octane fuel lodged just behind our seats. The pilots could not find the airstrip. Our fuel was now dangerously low. The pilots were thinking about how to abort in the desert.

A group from Doctors Without Borders realized we were in trouble. They drove their trucks to the strip illuminating it with their headlights. Marie-Noëlle was hysterical. Terry's hands dripped out of fear. The vehicles were lined up single file. The pilots weren't sure which side to land on. We exited the plane after a bouncy landing and noticed several men on camels and horses waiting to scavenge the wreck. (Or so I thought. Terry didn't agree with me.) They were disappointed. That night we were awakened with sounds of drums and cymbals and boisterous cheers as a large salt caravan of camels passed through town.

The second time I was truly scared was on a flight to Belize. See the full story in this book–Belize, Not Ready for Prime Time.

The third time was on a flight from Denver to Santa Fe in a small two-engine plane. We hit an air pocket and the plane nose-dived. Briefcases flew up in the air. The pilots' heads were between their knees. Terry and I reached across the aisle for each other's hand. We were wearing seatbelts and always will.

The fourth time was a real heart pounder. In October 1966, four of us who had been friends at the University of Minnesota flew to Eagle River, Wisconsin on the day that daylight savings time changed. Minnesota did not have a state law governing daylight savings time due to the classic urban vs. rural divisions in the Legislature. Farmers said the cows couldn't cope with the time change while city slickers wanted more evening playtime. Therefore no statewide law was in place. Each city chose its own time.

Pilot Bob Rolle (an old debating partner of mine), Gary Carlson, real estate developer hoping to look at some recreational property, Lyle Hurd, a sales guy for *Time-Life* and I took off in a rented University of Minnesota plane.

Bob checked the weather from his home in South St. Paul (no daylight savings time), drove through St Paul (daylight savings time) to Minneapolis (no daylight savings time), to pick me up in St. Louis Park (daylight savings time), to the Crystal Airport in north Minneapolis (no daylight savings time).

Bob rechecked the weather at my home (no mobile phones back then) but was off one hour (confusion about time zones) in his extrapolation for calculating the progress of a storm coming from the southeast. Rather than beating the storm by one hour we flew smack dab into the middle of it.

It was a dandy. Heavy rain and lots of bumps. Bob had to fly using instruments only. The plane, a Cessna 150, was not known for its electronic sophistication. Just when our paperwork said we should be getting out of the storm it became even more intense.

We couldn't see a thing except for flashes of lightning. All of us pulled our safety belts as tight as they would go. There was dead silence until the plane lurched so violently that Gary hit his head on something in the cockpit. It started to bleed. At the sight of blood Lyle, who was in the back seat with me, started to scream at Bob, the pilot.

Bob dropped the plane to treetop level and told us he was going to try to land. That was a problem because we were somewhere in the middle of the Chequamegon National Forest.

After ten more minutes of violent shaking and nothing but treetops in the mist and rain, we saw a small marsh. Bob told us to hold on and pray because he was going to drop it in.

Bob accomplished quite a plop down. He slowed the ground speed which triggered the alarm. He managed to drop the tail in the marsh water first. We slammed onto the belly of the plane and then up on its nose. It happened so fast we didn't have time to get more frightened than we already were.

Except for Gary's minor cut we were shaken but okay. We had to exit the plane while it was in its vertical position dropping down into the marsh. It was still raining like hell. As we stood in the water looking at the mess we realized we had no idea where we were or which direction was north. We failed to take the compass off the plane.

We walked for about 30 minutes through Wisconsin's thickest forest in a driving rain and were buoyed in spirit when we came to a gravel road. About 20 minutes later a farmer in a pickup truck came along and picked us up. We were four wet, cold entrepreneurs. He dropped us off just as it was getting dark at the Ford dealership in Ladysmith, Wisconsin. The rain had stopped but the wind was howling.

It took quite a while for the owner of the dealership to come from his home to meet us. He reluctantly rented us a vehicle we could use to get back to Minneapolis. He wasn't in the car rental business so it took a leap of faith for him to find a used car he could rent to us probably thinking he may never see it again.

We thanked him profusely and got into the car in front of his dealership. He was watching us through his glass door when I remembered that my briefcase was inside. While the rest of our group waited in the car, I ran through the wind, went inside, found my case, thanked him again and opened the big glass door of his showroom. A strong gust of wind ripped the door out of my hand and slammed it against the showroom window. The force was so great the handle of the door hit the window causing it to come crashing down.

It was a large window. Most of it was now in pieces on the grass and sidewalk. I remember glass in the flower beds. I didn't know what to say other than I'm sorry, I'll help clean it up. He swore at the situation, not at me, but told me that the last thing he wanted was for us to hang around. He asked us to leave.

What a day!

Terry, me, Fred and Marie-Noëlle Meyer trying to smile the day after a harrowing night landing in Timbuktu.

THE SUMPTER FAMILY OF KENTUCKY

A Model Of Self-Sufficiency

I HAD AN INCREDIBLY EASY TIME in the US Army. I was drafted into a peacetime army and sent to code school which kept me on as an instructor after graduation. I spent my full service in Kentucky.

A fellow soldier/instructor, Tom Mangum of Chicago, fell in love with a sweet girl from Whitesburg, Kentucky. Tom asked me to go with him to meet her family. Later my former wife and I hosted the family at their wedding in Louisville.

Visiting her family, the Sumpters, was my first exposure to Appalachia and real poverty. I'll never forget a man sitting on a porch of a run-down shanty with his eyeball hanging out.

The Sumpters lived out of town and were amazingly self-sufficient. Except for salt and wheat flour, they raised or extracted everything they needed. They made corn flour, owned animals for butchering or milking and ate a lot of squirrels. Mr. Sumpter took me squirrel hunting and had me fire his non-bored rifle. Without boring in the barrel, you had to learn the idiosyncrasies of the weapon. His rifle fired about a foot to the left at 50 yards and the bullet dropped about six inches. I now knew what Kentucky windage and Tennessee elevation meant.

They had an outhouse propped over a tributary of the Cumberland River. You could watch your own poop and paper (a catalog sheet, really) float down the river if you hurried.

Their mattresses and pillows were made from goose down and they heated the stove and house with coal from their own coal seam. To get the coal you had to lie on your back on a small flat sled on rails and propel yourself with your hands about 100 feet into the mountainside. The tunnel was only 32 inches high so your nose almost touched the ceiling. While lying on your back, you hammered and chipped coal into a bucket attached to the sled. Dirty and dangerous work. Mrs. Sumpter operated a hand air pump which blew fresh air into the tunnel through a perpendicular hose.

They had me go into the seam. I panicked. Mr. Sumpter had to pull me out by a rope attached to the foot of the sled.

I spent several weekends with the Sumpters, most without their future son-in-law, as I was now a friend of the family

Political jobs accounted for about 25% of the jobs in the county. Mr. Sumpter was a school bus driver (a political appointment) and it paid him $900 per year, his only cash income. I started a collection of very quaint local political posters. One poster showed an overweight man seated with his wife and seven children. The headline read, "I really need this job." He was running for deputy sheriff.

Mr. Sumpter arranged a trip for me into one of the new mines. I was stunned by the noise, dust, water (to hold the dust down) and the sense of danger. It is amazing what the human spirit can adapt to.

Mrs. Sumpter prepared a special breakfast for me on my last trip to the Sumpters. Corn muffins, maple syrup, biscuits in cream sauce, grits and squirrel. As an artistic touch, she served a large platter with a circle of little eyes looking up at me. You eat the heads of squirrels with a nutcracker.

Goodbye Appalachia. You broadened my vision.

THE MALL OF AMERICA

It Will Never Fly

I COULD NOT BELIEVE WHAT WAS HAPPENING. The impossible now seemed possible. The nation's largest shopping mall could become a reality in Minnesota, of all places.

The Ghermezian brothers, builders of a huge mall in Edmonton, Ontario, had combined with Melvin Simon and Associates of Indianapolis and the city of Bloomington to build the infrastructure for a 400-store mall with an indoor amusement park.

As head of the Minneapolis Downtown Marketing Committee and chair-elect of the Minneapolis Downtown Council, I was worried a supermall would kill business in the downtown area. John Borchert, professor of geography at the University of Minnesota and a retail specialist, projected we would become the most over retailed community in America. Mitsubishi of Japan was to provide the financing. It was a done deal.

One evening after a Council meeting, a group of us got together at

Murray's restaurant and commiserated. After a few drinks, I drummed up the idea to circulate a petition encouraging folks to go to the Mall of America but asking them not to buy anything for five years. Everyone laughed. Pat Murray typed up a simple petition, duplicated it and sent it around to all the tables in the restaurant. Almost everyone in the place signed it and wanted to buy us a drink.

Somehow the petition managed to get circulated outside of Murray's and soon signed versions started coming to Carmichael Lynch. (Ironically, the agency was on the list to make a presentation for the Mall's advertising contract.)

The *Star Tribune* got wind of it and ran a short story that caused more petitions to pour in. Soon after I had a visit from a PR officer from Mel Simon's company. She offered to fly me to Edmonton on Mr. Simon's jet to see its mall so I could learn about what I was foolishly trying to interfere with.

I declined the offer. Shortly after her visit an attorney for Mel Simon and Associates served me with a cease and desist order. I was accused of trying to harm the Mall financially for the betterment of my land holdings in downtown Minneapolis.

I immediately called my attorney, David Bennett, and read the document to him. He paused and then said, "unless you have a pathological need to lose money, sign the order and drop the whole matter."

Why were they so upset? It turns out the financing they claimed to have had hit some snags. The last thing they needed was a grassfire of locals signing a petition against the Mall.

I was, as was Professor Borchert, sure the Mall would fail if it was ever built. We held a contest to see what the failed Mall could be used for in the future. The winning entry was to make the Mall a living zoo for failed developers.

I was beaten but I got back at them. I refused to ever set foot in the Mall of America. And I haven't. I didn't even visit son-in-law Kurt's store in the Mall or the grand opening of the largest Archiver's store (I had a substantial investment in the company). I sure showed them.

Of course, some of my friends have sent me clippings now touting the Mall of America as the leading tourist destination in America.

More visitors than Disney World.

Shows how smart I was.

In September of 2020 the Mall was in arrears for four payments on the largest real estate loan in America. Covid-19 restrictions hit them hard.

MAESTRO OF MINNESOTA

Give Me The Baton

ACCORDING TO *Amazing Minnesota*, there are only six cities in the world with two internationally ranked orchestras. An orchestra must record and regularly tour internationally to be so ranked.

The Twin Cities are blessed to be home to the St. Paul Chamber Orchestra and the Minnesota Symphony Orchestra. Both tour and record regularly.

It's highly likely that only one person in the world has conducted both of these renowned orchestras (except professional conductors, of course). That would be me!

In the early 80s Terry and I attended a fancy social event–the Minnesota Symphony Ball. This was my first event of this type. I even had to wear a tux.

As part of the event an opportunity to conduct the orchestra was offered for auction. Many big spenders bid up the chance to conduct. A friend of mine, Frank Skillern, an American Express executive, wanted to conduct and was prepared to pay.

As the bidding was ending, Frank instructed me to make the penultimate final bid. I couldn't afford it but he planned to overbid me at the last minute. He promised to take me out.

I made the bid, expecting Frank to call out a raise. "Going once, going twice..." I looked around. No Frank. "Sold to the man in the green bow tie." The conductor beckoned me to climb the stairs. I was worried. At each step I looked for Frank. He was in the men's room. I was stuck.

I panicked as I was handed the baton. I didn't enjoy conducting the *Stars and Stripes Forever*. It should have been fun, it wasn't.

Again, an auction, this time for an opportunity to conduct the St. Paul Chamber Orchestra. Terry was the winning bidder and gave me the baton for my birthday. No tired but true *Stars and Stripes* for me. I wanted to demonstrate my conducting skills on Copeland's *Appalachian Spring*. Hugh Wolfe insisted I practice with the orchestra. The first rehearsal was a disaster. There was a transition in the composition I just couldn't figure out. I listened to the SPCO recording over and over again. I knew I could do it.

The night came to conduct. I was confident and up for the challenge. As I took the podium Hugh Wolfe sat in a corner, out of sight, and told the orchestra if I got in trouble to follow him and not me. "No way," I said to the band while they watched my lips, and I gestured to where Hugh was sitting, "Watch me, not him." It worked.

The following year I bid for Terry to conduct the St. Paul Chamber Orchestra. She did a superb rendition of the *Stars and Stripes Forever*.

Terry conducting the SPCO. *Me directing* Appalachian Spring.

Fritz showing Terry his antique vampire-slaying box.

FRITZ

A Weird Collection

ONE OF THE MOST UNUSUAL HOMES I have ever been in was owned by a Minnesota boy, Fritz Scholder, born in Breckenridge, MN.

Fritz was a famous Native American artist...one of the most successful. Terry and I own four of his works including a large canvas titled *Man and Dog*.

Fritz lived most of his life in New Mexico and Arizona. He invited us to his studio in Scottsdale after we expressed an interest in buying one of his paintings. We finalized the deal in his beautiful large studio and then crossed the drive to his home.

A large bat (vampire?) hung over the front door. As we entered we saw a nude woman lying face down on the floor with her head in her hands. It was a very, very life-like sculpture. Around the door were macabre symbols of death, old (illegal) Egyptian tomb death masks and shrunken heads. A large sarcophagus was positioned in the center of the room. A life-size stuffed buffalo was the headboard of his bed.

He kept an original vampire box from Transylvania on his sideboard. It was an old wooden box stuffed with a crucifix, pistol, hammer, stake, garlic and silver bullet. Everything to kill or ward off a vampire. A two-headed goat was hanging on the wall in the kitchen. The bizarre was everywhere. The back yard had perfect green grass, a small swimming pool, furniture and water glasses from the fifties. Everything perfect.

Fritz told us he had authorized four trusted friends to purchase weird things for him sight unseen.

His house was filled with hundreds of objects and none of his paintings.

Symbols of death were everywhere in his house.

Nelson Atkins Museum of Art Bloch Building.

FARTBURG

Spicy BBQ

TERRY AND I WENT TO KANSAS CITY for "little" Tommy Zavoral's wedding. He was marrying into a fine family and a fun weekend was in store. We had an afternoon to kill after dining on Kansas City's finest and spiciest barbecue, so we went to a well-known museum–the Nelson Atkins Museum of Art Bloch Building.

The building was very modern and stark, dark stone inside and out, high ceilings with exceptionally large rooms that felt a bit lonely.

I heard a loud fart as Terry descended a flight of stairs into the first large gallery. It was especially loud because the room was empty and the sound reverberated off the stone walls. Fortunately no one heard it.

On the second flight of stairs, it happened again and we both laughed. Laughing brought on the third very loud fart.

I quickly moved away from Terry. As she started toward me every step brought on another retort. More laughter and more noise. I wanted some distance from her because the few people who were in the gallery were looking at us. I went around a corner and could hear her coming. With every step, she farted. She finally quieted down so I thought it was safe to be with her. Not so.

The noise returned with gusto when Terry asked a guard where the restrooms were and suddenly realized that the guard was a realistic sculpture of a guard. She started laughing and farting all over again.

I ran away from her and tried to get on the elevator before she came around the corner. I didn't want to be seen with her.

I met her outside the main door. Neither of us can remember seeing one piece of art other than the guard sculpture.

EVELYN'S ASHES

Tippy Canoe

I THINK SHE GOT BACK AT US. For what reason I don't know for we loved that 92-year-old crabby doll.

Evelyn Drieman lived at 2 Park Lane in Minneapolis in the smallest house on the block. A former schoolteacher and wife of the man she adored, John Drieman.

John and Evelyn's son, John Jr., a bright but eccentric guy, lived in New Jersey (has since moved to Nova Scotia) and was in the specialty magazine publishing business, like those kitchen and bath remodeling magazines you see in magazine racks.

John knew we were close to Evelyn and had her to our home for Thanksgiving and Christmas dinners. I also visited her almost every night when I took Cork out for his walk. One day when John was on one of his infrequent visits to Minnesota he dropped into our home and was bowled over by our new kitchen. He talked us into being featured in one of his kitchen design magazines. It was a nice story.

Death was a relief for Evelyn. She was in horrible shape and could not stand or walk erect. As her pain increased so did her temper. She was impossible but we hung in there with her.

Evelyn died in March of 2008. Terry and I held a memorial service for her at our home. It was well attended and included some of her old teacher friends. One of them, Joanne, was her regular Sunday night visitor. They often watched British mysteries on PBS together.

Joanne was very dour and severe looking. She stood about six feet tall with her hair up in a bun like an old volleyball player. She was brilliant and sought after as an author and consultant.

John asked if Evelyn's ashes could be kept at our home until summer when he would come back and fulfill her wishes to have them sprinkled in Cedar Lake right behind her home. We put them in a wooden chest at the foot of the basement stairs along with our dear dog Cork's ashes.

John arrived in late August and arranged to have Joanne be a part of the burial ceremony. Shortly before Joanne arrived at our house, I took John downstairs and showed him the box where we kept the ashes.

We were stunned when I opened the box and saw that her ashes were not in the box. John thought I was joking. I asked if he possibly took them. No, of course not was the answer. John still thought I was joking. I convinced him I wasn't. We had to do something before Joanne arrived. John could handle the loss of the ashes with good humor but Joanne definitely could not. I suggested we substitute some of my brother Tommy's ashes. He laughed and said no way. I was prepared to face the dour dame when I spotted Evelyn's box of ashes in one of the wine boxes in the basement. Whew!

After a couple of glasses of wine and a simple dinner, John, Joanne and I took the ashes down to the lake and prepared to get into a canoe. It was a very fancy new "explorers" model I borrowed from Bill Bowen down the block.

I got in first and moved the nose of the canoe up on the beach a foot or two. Joanne was dressed in a severe black turtleneck with matching slacks. She wrapped a black silk scarf around her neck. Hair up, camera in hand she got in the canoe and almost tipped it. John pushed the canoe out and got in the bow. I assumed John knew about canoes. Wrong.

He stood too erect and lunged in dumping all three of us in two feet of water. I laughed. John laughed. Joanne scowled. She was pissed. Her camera got wet as well as the bun on her head and all of her clothes. Terry could barely convince her to put her clothes in our dryer and wear a bathrobe while she waited.

John and I paddled off into the sunset (literally) sprinkling ashes, laughing.

Evelyn enjoyed her final moments.

Former Palestinian Prime Minister Salam Fayyad.

WORLD LEADERS TOUR

Benjamin's Explosion

A brilliant idea:

– *Retain the services of a well-known tv personality*
– *Retain the services of well-known Israeli experts*
– *Advertise an Israeli tour that provides interviews with important leaders from Israel and Palestine*
– *Name the tour World Leaders Forum*
– *Tell the leaders of both Israel and Palestine you have a* VIP *group of leaders from America who deserve and expect access to leadership*

Terry and I have always sought special insights into foreign countries. The World Leaders Tour was exactly what we were looking for. Of course we wanted to see the religious sights but politics was our passion.

The tour group leaders would be Sam Donaldson, formerly of ABC *News*, Aaron David Miller, a well-known and frequently quoted expert on Israeli-Palestinian affairs, the editor of *Foreign Affairs* magazine and an acclaimed professor of foreign affairs at Bard College. Former publisher of the *Minneapolis Star Tribune* Roger Parkingson and wife Mureen were our traveling companions.

The tour company planned on a group of 60. Only 30 of us paid the high-priced fees and our group was certainly not composed of world leaders.

Every day started with a lecture based on the reading materials given to us the day before. The lecturers were high ranking officials in government, academia and the military. The afternoons were spent visiting sites and meeting with top Israeli officials.

Among many, we met with former President Perez, the son of the assassinated Prime Minister Rabin, the Israeli head of security (who took us on a tour of the extensive electrical fencing system separating Israel from Palestine) and a leading member of the Knesset (the Israeli parliament).

We visited Yasser Arafat's tomb, met with Salam Fayyad, the Palestinian prime minister and Dr. Saeb Erekat, the Palestinian chief negotiator.

We had a security briefing from an Israeli major who wore a flak jacket, not to protect himself from the Palestinians but from extreme right-wing Israelis. The right-wing killed Prime Minister Rabin because he sought compromise with the Palestinians. The mayor was a peace negotiator and skilled at compromise. Things were especially tense when George Mitchell, former US Senator and the US envoy to the peace negotiations, landed in Tel Aviv.

Our final meeting was with the temperamental President Benjamin Netanyahu. About 20 of us sat at a round table headed by the President. We were told to ask only one or two questions. It was determined that Sam Donaldson would start with a softball question followed by Terry who would ask a more controversial one. Terry was selected because Netanyahu would not see her as threatening. Terry's question dealt with the most explosive issue currently in the press, Israel's expansion into Palestinian land.

Netanyahu blew up. He slammed his fists on the table, ranted, raved and suggested she did not know what she was talking about. Terry did not flinch but kept a calm smile. It drove him crazy.

The meeting ended and so did the company. World Leaders Forum went out of business without a full complement of 60 well-paying clients.

In Argentine wine country with Manuel and Irene Bayon, in better days.

DON'T CRY FOR ME

Turbulent Argentina

WHILE ATTENDING THE ANNUAL MEETINGS of the American Association of Advertising Agencies over the years, Terry and I met several agency people who became friends. Often the relationship was cemented by my very social and outgoing wife. People loved her and she was always interested in people from other countries who attended the event.

Manuel Bayon ran a medium-sized agency in Buenos Aires that specialized in working for non-US dominated local companies. Not McDonald's but the local alternative. It was a good niche for Manuel. Whenever we saw him and his wife, Irene, sitting alone we always invited them to sit with us. They were appreciative of Terry's act of kindness. Manuel spoke very little English but his wife was fluent and a partner in an Argentine consumer research company. We liked them both very much and developed a friendship that went beyond the Association meetings. They visited us in Santa Fe and later Manuel arranged for me to speak to the South American Advertising Association.

He took care of us on our visit to Argentina. His office was very contemporary, their apartment in the city lovely and they had a nice home on a golf course. They also had a cabin cruiser on the Rio de la Plata. Manuel and Irene had it all including a cute son, Nico.

Then came disaster.

The Argentine financial system crashed and no one could withdraw money from the banks. Many banks had no money and its depositors were uninsured. I knew that Manuel would be affected and talked with him more than once about his condition. He said he was finally going to give up on Argentina and move back to his childhood country of Spain. He said he and Irene were going to start over. Over the next few months nothing changed. I suspected he didn't have the cash to make the trip and get reestablished in Madrid. I asked him three times if I could lend him money and he declined. On the fourth time, he asked if I could wire $10,000 to a bank in Spain. He said he would pay it back as soon as he got his feet on the ground.

Manuel did start over and became a partner with an older man in a research company in Madrid. They lived in one of the new cities that ringed Madrid. Two years later he contacted us and said he was able to pay us back but we had to come to Spain to collect. Of course we went and were hosted again by the two of them for two weeks. One of the highlights was visiting his family in Asturias, a northern Spanish province on the ocean. It was great fun, gave us a chance to see the art museum at Bilbo and have the best lunch of our life at a three-star restaurant called Akalara.

On our last night with the family Manuel made a touching speech about our friendship and how we saved his life. He was happy even though he knew he would never be able to own a home in Spain or drive a new car because of the expense. He also learned that Argentinians were viewed as immigrants and subtly discriminated against. It was a joyful and tearful dinner. Nico was a talented child and a great student. At the end of our dinner Manuel gave us an envelope containing $10,000. Terry and I had already planned to give the money back. We didn't want to embarrass them so we returned it to Nico for his college education fund. It was not their money, it was Nico's. There were tears around the table.

As Manuel dropped us off at the airport the next day we said goodbye and started into the terminal. As I looked back I saw Manuel walking down the sidewalk with his back to us. I noticed he had his handkerchief in his hand and was sobbing.

They eventually moved back to Argentina. They just couldn't make it in Spain.

We went to Patagonia in 2013 and stopped in Buenos Aires for a couple of days to visit with Manuel, Irene, Nico and the latest member of their family, Paloma. Always the perfect host Manuel arranged for us to stay at a friend's home located on a beautiful golf course just outside of Buenos Aires.

Manuel was in the service/retail electronics business and Irene was working part-time in the consumer research business. We had the feeling his current lifestyle was less than it had been in Madrid and much less than during his advertising career.

We had a pleasant time and got to know the children a little better. Nico was on the verge of becoming a teenager and quite proud of his English fluency.

With all their ups and downs Manuel kept his great smile and graciousness. But his eyes looked sad. Mine would be too.

BELIZE

Not Ready For Prime Time

THIS WAS A TRIP that should not have happened. I heard Belize was the country of the future for sun-seeking Americans. Reasonably priced and ready for take-off.

It wasn't. Still twenty years away.

Terry and I were interested in seeing the ancient ruins of Tikal in Guatemala. We planned to spend three days in the jungle and three days snorkeling off the coast.

First problem: getting there.

I knew we were going to have a problem when the cabin attendant approached Terry and me and asked us to step into the galley. She told us the landing gear wouldn't lock. We most likely would be forced to make a belly landing. We were given instructions on how to open the door in case she wasn't available. Terry's hands dripped with sweat. I went back to my seat and continued reading my book.

We were diverted to the airport in Cancun, Mexico rather than the small one in Belize City. As I looked out the window I could see scores of fire trucks and ambulances waiting along the runway. This might be our big day.

The landing gear held. We were safe but the plane had to be repaired and a part flown in. Trouble was we were in Mexico without permission to land or stay. They herded us into a small, hot unpleasant room for almost three hours. Then a bus carted us off to a horrible hotel an hour away over the worst road in the Western Hemisphere.

The hotel wasn't prepared for 180 guests. It took forever to get us to our rooms. We were later summoned to dinner which was pasta with Chef Boyardee sauce. No flavor. Lukewarm.

Off to bed only to be awakened at 3:30 a.m. to board the bus back to the airport and off once again to Belize City.

We missed our connection to Tikal and had no other way to get there. We were stuck in Belize City until a broken-down cab hauled us two hours away into the jungle over another pothole-ridden road.

The resort was in the jungle and deserved at least one star. I swam in a jungle river and Terry and I toured a natural medicine facility in the woods. An American herbalist showed us all the herbs available in the jungle and the wondrous things they could do for the body. Terry was hooked and bought several packages. We never used any of them because of preparation time and taste.

Off to the coast to snorkel. Again, the hotel was a one-star. The guide for the swim was sick so his grandson was the substitute. He took three of us out to a large coral field and off we went. It was spectacular. He told us to follow him through a narrow opening to swim back to the boat. It was very choppy. So choppy we were all bleeding from scraping against the coral once we were in the middle of the reef.

We could not make it back to the boat by continuing forward so we had to swim back the same way we came in, bleeding a lot. As I looked down through my mask I saw a large shark lying on the bottom. I panicked and my breathing became very irregular. I thought for sure it would smell the blood and make a movie out of us. Turns out it was a harmless but large nurse shark.

When we got back to the boat the guide squeezed lime juice on our open sores. I had about twenty cuts, including on my head.

The country was not ready for tourism but it was ready for large-scale farming. Mennonite farmers from the US cultivated over 100,000 acres of farmland. As we passed through the farmland I thought I was in southern Minnesota.

The story does not end. Weeks later I started to run a fever for a few days at a time. This went on for quite some time. I was exhausted. The doctors couldn't figure out what the problem was until I said I was swimming in a jungle river. Yes. That's it. They sent my blood sample to the CDC in Atlanta and it came back with the answer.

It was not a parasite from swimming in the river.

Coral poisoning. Goodbye Belize. You weren't right for us.

Professor David Welsh in South African wine country.

DAVID OF CAPE TOWN

A Lucky Guest

IT WAS WELL BELOW ZERO ON A FRIDAY night when Bob Gale called to ask a favor. Bob, an old friend of Terry's and a graduate and trustee of Carleton College, found out while attending a winter graduation event that the commencement speaker did not have a place to stay until Monday when his flight departed. Someone at Carleton had screwed up and Bob was hoping Terry and I could help mitigate an embarrassing situation with our hospitality.

We agreed with a little apprehension. This unexpected guest could ruin our entire weekend. The only thing we knew about our guest was his name was David Welsh and he was a professor at the University of Cape Town in South Africa.

David arrived on our doorstep at 7 p.m. with a small suitcase and no overcoat. He looked uneasy as we introduced ourselves. David immediately asked us to go on with our weekend plans and he would be "just fine."

He accepted my offer of a bit of scotch and after the first sip we could tell he might be quite interesting. By the second scotch we knew he was more than interesting. We were due at a dinner and asked the hosts if we could include him. David was a hit. Funny, engaging and clearly at ease with our friends.

The next morning David wanted to get outdoors in the snow. This was his first experience in really cold weather and really deep snow. We outfitted him in boots, snow pants, hat, gloves and a warm coat.

David was fascinated by our environment and wanted to stay out all day. I remember him walking across Lake Calhoun in knee-deep snow.

We spent the weekend showing him the Twin Cities, walking, dining, talking and learning a great deal about South Africa. His wife, Virginia Van Fleet, who David said looked strikingly like Terry, was a leading authority on AIDS in South Africa and had recently written a best selling book on the subject. David was a prominent member of the anti-apartheid movement in South Africa and was a well-respected political scientist on the Cape Town faculty.

Both of us thoroughly enjoyed the weekend with David and were sad to see him leave on Monday. As we dropped him at the airport he was insistent that we soon be his guests in South Africa.

Two years later we planned a trip to South Africa to visit the famous Kruger Game Reserve accompanied by our dear friend Nancy Speer. A visit to Cape Town was on our itinerary and we alerted David of our trip.

David insisted he was to be our guide in Cape Town and its surroundings. Our day started with breakfast at the most popular restaurant in town. The place was jammed and everyone there seemed to know him. It was the meeting place for all the top politicians, including the Prime Minister Botha. Everyone, including the Prime Minister, dropped by our table.

We had just finished our meal when a hush came over the large room. Everyone started to whisper. News just broke that President Mugabe of Zimbabwe ordered the confiscation of farmlands owned by white farmers.

The worry in the room was that South Africa could be next. David did not let the news change his plans to drive us through the countryside for two days. Huge, rich farmlands and vineyards near Stellenbosch, touring the prosperous Afrikaner towns, gorgeous seashores and the beautiful city of Cape Town was much more than we could ever have expected.

David told us of a chilling dimension of apartheid. During that desperate period, one was classified as White, Black or Mixed. All three were segregated to their own section of the city.

A colleague at the university accused another professor of being of mixed blood. It seemed unlikely given his red hair and tenured position. At that time anyone could accuse someone else of being mixed if they paid $2,400 (SA equivalent) for the genealogy search.

The red-haired professor was proven to be of mixed blood. He was forced to resign not only his position at the university but to sell his home and move into the mixed section of town. And of course he could no longer be married to his white wife.

The dirty irony of this story was the accuser got the desirable tenured position on the faculty. We had heard of the great injustices apartheid dealt but the ability to accuse and remove was a diabolical extension of an evil society.

David was shunned during apartheid as he bore witness to its evil. When apartheid ended David became a hero for his courageous stance against that evil.

Not a bad ending for an unexpected Friday night guest.

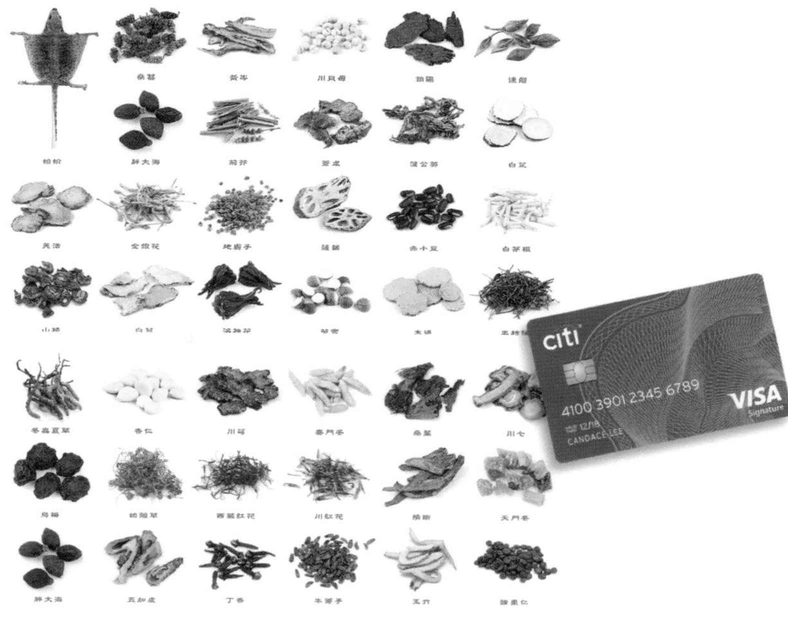

CHINESE MEDICINE

Bring Your Credit Card

WE TRAVELED IN CHINA with two wonderful couples who were good Democrats. Thank goodness because all of us chose to watch the Al Gore/George Bush debate instead of going to the Great Wall. Except for that, we ate everything, did everything and saw everything we could in two weeks.

Since it was a highly customized trip we could ask to tour anything of interest to us including a Chinese hospital. One area in the hospital was dedicated to acupuncture. Dozens of people were lying on mats with suction cups on their backs. Patients in other rooms had needles inserted into their bodies. Who knows what was going on in other areas we were not allowed to enter.

At the end of the hospital tour we were taken to a classroom and given a demonstration of electricity in the body. A young handsome attendant was given a small light bulb to hold while doing rapid deep breathing. After a minute or so the bulb started to dimly light. We were given the bulb to examine.

The most senior doctor among a group of four gave us a lecture on Chinese medicine and its amazing benefits. He then asked anyone who had a sore spot or an injury to allow the doctors to use electricity to cure them. One by one several got up while I videotaped the "cure." Everyone excitedly said the electricity worked.

Then the doctor talked about herbs and roots that were almost miraculously medicinal. Where could we buy such wonders?

Bingo! The magic question.

Out of each "doctor's" white coat pocket came a credit card charging machine. They were more than ready. I videoed the lambs being led to slaughter in the land of hope.

Marna, one of our companions, spent $1,100 on the magic potions.

I suspect she never used even one of them.

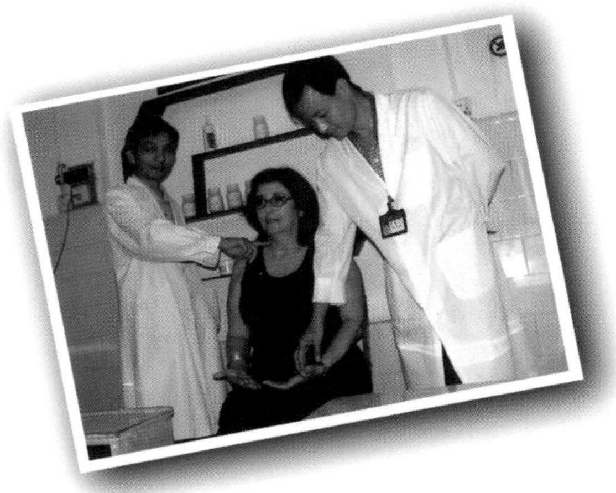

Chinese doctors curing a sore spot on our friend, Candace Lee.

Terry was about to discover a real Turkish bath.

TURKISH BATH

A Dinner Embarrassment

We met many interesting people over the years at Jumby Bay in Antigua. People tended to return at the same time each year as did we. Among these folks were two eccentric Brits, Bill and Vivien. One year we were talking about what they had done recently and they extolled us about having been to Petra in Jordan. They found Petra so entrancing they decided to go back to see more of its wonders. They had recently booked another trip to Petra on the Concorde. Terry and I were fascinated by their descriptions. Bill thought the flight on the Concorde was fully booked. He asked if we would be willing to join them if it wasn't. Yes, of course. He contacted his travel agent in Scotland and reserved the last two seats on the plane for us.

We met Bill and Vivien in London before we departed for Jordan. Only then did we discover that Bill, a Scotsman, was the CEO of a large conglomerate. Vivien and he traveled in the same circles as Winston Churchill's son, Randolph. We ran into Randolph at a posh restaurant where we were all having lunch not far from Buckingham Palace. We also learned that Bill and Vivien lived a couple of blocks away from the palace and paid a fortune to park their car in a garage nearby. Funny how nondescript bathing suits disguise one's fortunes.

We flew on the Concorde. This was the second time we had been on the plane. Its cramped quarters made the flight physically uncomfortable. And because the Concorde was restricted from flying at supersonic speeds over populated land we had only a brief experience of Mach speed over the Mediterranean Sea. No wonder the Concorde failed.

Our group stayed at one of the best hotels in Amman, Jordan. Terry was a little uneasy in this environment. She cautioned me not to say anything in public places so the locals would think we were British. (A few years later a bomb was detonated in the same hotel in one of the public areas where a wedding was taking place. Many people were killed.)

I was happy there was a pool in the hotel but not happy with the man in it. He wore a swim cap and goggles and came up out of the water right beside me. He asked me in a threatening way "Are you Jewish?" I swam to the other side of the pool and got out.

After a day in Amman, we flew to Petra where our accommodations were unique. We stayed in an authentic Arab village that had been converted into a small boutique hotel.

We spent a day and a half exploring Petra, the Red Rose city. Petra was a trading center of some significance in the first century A.D. It was carved into red stone cliffs in the desert and was protected by a long winding narrow passageway to the entrance of the city. After walking some distance in narrow darkened tunnels, you are awestruck as you enter the city by the façade of the Treasury. Magnificent structures dot the cliffs on all sides of the city. It is rumored that Moses' brother was buried at Petra. You could spend days there exploring all its magnificence.

Besides going to Petra, our group was taken by train to Wadi Rum, an isolated desolate area of the desert in southern Jordan for an elaborate lunch. While on the train, a band of horsemen came alongside and "kidnapped" a passenger, placing her on the back of one of the galloping horses. At first, they were going to "kidnap" Terry but decided that she was too heavy for the horse...much to her dismay.

When we returned to the village that evening, we opted to take a Turkish bath. Neither of us had done this before. I went first. A young man summoned me after I had waited about 15 minutes in a large, tiled sauna-like room. I found myself naked in a shower where the young man scrubbed me down with a big brush, front and back. I then retired wrapped in warm towels to another tiled room filled with plush pillows to drink tea and wait for Terry. I knew what was coming. What I didn't know was that the same man who scrubbed me was also scrubbing her...fully naked.

She was furious at me for not telling her what was coming so she could avoid it. Too bad, Terry. She was very embarrassed but not as embarrassed as she was that night at dinner. Our waiter was the same guy who cleaned up her act.

The Turkish bath was part of the experience in Jordan but seeing the Treasury at Petra and to bathe in the Dead Sea were extraordinary experiences as well.

Climbing up the interior of the pyramid was a bit claustrophobic.

TIGHT SPACES

Try Not To Panic

I AM GENERALLY NOT CLAUSTROPHOBIC, although in recent years I've noted a certain nervousness when I'm in a cramped space with too many people.

However, three times in my life I came close to panicking.

The first tight space was when Terry and I were off the coast of a small island in the Galapagos Islands. Mateo, the captain of our six-person sailboat, encouraged me to join him and go night diving for lobsters.

He gave me a metal mesh glove with a small flashlight attached to it with Velcro. I was to use the gloved hand as protection to pick up the lobster. We swam about a block to the rocky coastline. Mateo told me we would have to dive under some rocks and come up in caves on the other side. He said I would have to hold my breath for about a minute.

Then he left me to go under. It was no problem going under the rock. I thought I was going to come up into a large chamber. Wrong. As I popped up, I banged my head on the low ceiling, panicked, flailed about and knocked the flashlight off the glove. It settled on the sea bottom right next to a large lobster. I knew the light was valuable and I had to retrieve it. It seemed close. Wrong again. I couldn't make it, popped back up and hit my head again.

This time I didn't panic. I realized I was disoriented and didn't know which direction the opening was. Had to get the flashlight. I used the low ceiling as something to push off from and with my feet on the roof I shot down to the bottom and grabbed the flashlight and the lobster. Smart guy. No big deal. But now I knew why the light was attached to the gloved hand because I found it impossible to swim under the rock and back out to sea holding a flashlight in one hand and a lobster in the other. I dropped the lobster. Never again.

The second time was at the Pyramids in Egypt. We arrived at the Great Pyramid early in the day when there weren't a lot of other tourists. We saw some people coming out the side of the Pyramid about one-fourth of the way up. There was an opening in the wall with steps leading up to it. We learned there was an interior crypt in the middle of the Pyramid. You could reach the crypt room if you bent low and climbed a great number of stairs. I had to give it a try. Terry took a pass. Just looking at the hole was enough to cause anyone with even the slightest bit of claustrophobia to faint.

I crawled in and up. The very narrow shaft was dimly lit every fifty feet or so. In a few minutes, two people were coming down. We had to squeeze by each other in a very personal way. It seemed like it took forever to reach the tomb. When I got there, I could barely see the room. It was about 30-feet by 40-feet and 20-feet high. In the middle, a group of people were holding hands and chanting while looking down at a crypt. They invited me to join them. I did. They chanted something strange while looking about six feet down at one of their group lying prostrate at the bottom of the crypt. This chanting and circling of the crypt continued until everyone had a chance to go down into the hole. Soon it was my turn. Once again, what the heck? So, there I lay looking up at a bunch of dimly lit Brits chanting some strange incantation.

Damn, I thought to myself. I'm from Belle Plaine, Minnesota. What would my mother think of this?

Then there was Vietnam. Terry and I spent three weeks in Vietnam with a guide who was also our driver. We went from Hanoi to the southern delta of the Mekong.

At the war memorial/museum in Cu Chi we were shown the tunnels that the Viet Cong used so well to defeat the US. There was an underground room rigged as a hospital and an underground staff meeting room. I wanted to see and experience more of the tunnel system.

Our guide arranged for a special tour normally not on the program. We took a short jeep ride and met a young man who spoke some English. He took me down a tunnel which forked into another tunnel that dropped down again sharply. I was starting to get nervous, breathing heavily and perspiring. I wanted out. He showed me how the Viet Cong could protect themselves from gassing and flooding. A wall could be quickly built using bricks, mud and a small piece of canvas or rubber, about the size of the tunnel. He said the Americans tried everything to ruin the tunnels and anyone in them.

Now I'm starting to panic. The guide noticed it and told me not to worry. A few yards ahead there was a place I could stick my head outside. He removed the cover of weeds and brush and let me breathe fresh air. Once I saw how close I was to the surface I started to relax.

The tour ended close to where we began. Near the exit there were a series of small rooms used to store weapons and ammo. The Viet Cong learned in an attack they could travel much faster through the tunnels if they didn't have to carry their weapons. They would be given a fully equipped weapon as they exited. The guide said it was organized so one of every ten soldiers was given a heavy weapon, mortar or machine gun.

Now I know how and why we lost the war.

I was more than glad to see Terry waiting in the museum.

Taj Mahal *Angkor Wat*

STUNNING SITES

Taj Mahal, Petra, Angkor Wat

Some iconic structures, sculptures or art become cliché as they are so often cited in brochures and news stories.

I had seen so many photos of the Taj Mahal I knew I would be disappointed when I saw the real thing in Agra, India. Instead I was stunned by the temple's beauty as I entered the gate and caught my first glimpse.

The same thing happened when we caught our first glimpse of Angkor Wat in Cambodia. Terry and I were able to scamper to the top and look around the vast temple area. Today all climbing is prohibited due to wear and tear on the ancient stones.

The ancient Jordanian town of Petra is hidden behind a quarter mile of twisting narrow gorge with 300-foot stone cliffs on either side. This defensive entrance, called the Siq, kept the marauders and Roman legions out. Heavy shadows give way to a brilliant slit of sunshine, showing a small portion of the Treasury in Petra. I was in awe. How did they carve this masterpiece out of pink sandstone?

Other remarkable memories:

– *Chapel of Sainte-Chapelle in Paris*
– *Blue Mosque in Turkey*
– *Jewel encrusted carriages in the Hermitage in St. Petersburg*
– *Iguazu Falls in Brazil*
– *Chaco Canyon in New Mexico*
– *Torres del Paine in Patagonia*
– *The Dogon country in Mali*
– *A large herd of wild horses chasing our train in the moonlight in Mongolia.*

Each of the 60 plus countries we have visited have sites that form wonderful visual memories, but these were the best.

Petra, Jordan

Terracotta warriors in Xian, China.

LIVERPOOL

A Stylish Show

Terry was named a fellow of the European Community in 1982. This was a big deal and allowed the two of us to travel to Europe in grand style paid for by the Europeans. The purpose of her fellowship was to learn about urban renewal and alternative energy projects in Europe. We met with government officials and project managers in Great Britain, France and Germany and took in the sights along the way.

Two events stand out. The lord mayor of London and his frail wife hosted us one afternoon. He was a large blustery man who had worked as a kid for a year in Minnesota. His wife was so thin you could see the veins in her arms and legs. Both the mayor and his wife wore the symbolic mace, the necklace of office, a huge chain with large keys attached to it. Each necklace must have weighed about 40 pounds. As a proper hostess, the dear lady rose to get us a cup of tea, but the weight of her necklace was too much. She fell back into her chair. An attendant came over and lifted her necklace as she rose again.

The second highlight was our time in Liverpool, home of the Beatles. Terry was to attend a conference on the Liverpool waterfront redevelopment plan and a special event was arranged just for me, the spouse.

Often when Terry and I traveled to foreign countries on business, our hosts would assume that Dr. Saario was a man while Lee was his wife.

I did not know what occasion had been planned for me in Liverpool. I suspected something was amiss when my escort arrived to take me to the event. She seemed uncomfortable. I soon found out why. Another host explained to me my special event was a fashion show highlighting the work of the women of Liverpool–showcasing their fashion designs and seamstress abilities.

We entered a large hall jammed with mannequins and about a hundred women in their 50s and 60s. They parted like the Red Sea when they saw me. No one wanted to talk to me. The ladies backed away as my guides walked me though the exhibit.

They simply did not know what to do with me. They finally decided to suspend the inspection of the work and take me directly to lunch.

It was an uncomfortable lunch. She was a he and he was a she.

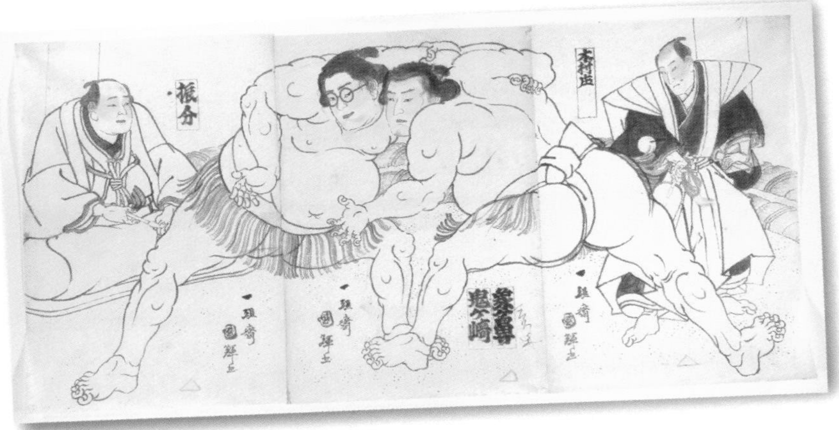

JAPAN MAN

No Sumo Today

TERRY AND I FIRST VISITED JAPAN with the Minneapolis College of Art and Design around 1988. It piqued our interest, so when Terry had an opportunity to apply for a Japan Society fellowship in 2000 she did and it was granted. We were going to Japan for three months.

I was not going to be at the agency for 90 days. I was apprehensive. My sense of self was wrapped up in the agency. It also would be the first time I had not worked since seventh grade.

While in Japan our base of operation was a lovely place called the I-House (International House) located in the Roppongi area of Tokyo. It was reserved for Japan Society members, scholars and honored visitors. Our room was sparse but had a beautiful garden view.

During the first few weeks, Terry would go to work at the foundation which sponsored her while I was left trying to fill the day. In those first few days, I wandered without purpose, trying to understand the basics of the Japanese language and life. I walked miles each day, covering most of the area around Roppongi. There weren't any street signs and finding my way around was difficult.

I slowly adjusted and started beginning Japanese language classes while Terry worked. Around the fourth week we started to take trips into rural areas of Japan and other major cities. Everywhere we went we were formally greeted and escorted. We usually had a car and driver/translator. Invariably, the people meeting us would assume that I was Dr. Saario. They were embarrassed when they discovered their mistake.

Terry gave speeches everywhere we went, usually about economic development or the women's movement in the US. I just listened. Finally some men asked me what I did. I told them that I was a "housu hosbando des" or "house husband" in English. They were surprised by the answer. They asked if I did the laundry, cooked and cleaned. I said with great emphasis, "iee laundry" (no laundry).

When back in Tokyo, I continued to take language lessons, walked in the afternoons and attended sumo matches. They were intriguing and helped me understand the cultural attraction sumo holds for the Japanese.

We attended a fall festival in the small mountainous town of Oguni. Other than the English language teacher we were the only gaijin (foreigners) in the town. We were invited to a home-stay in the mayor's house. He was proud of his new ToTo (toilet)...the kind with sprays and blowers and a warm seat. He came into the bathroom while I was using it to show me all the levers and buttons.

While watching the festival's local sumo match, Terry and the mayor thought I should try wrestling since I enjoyed the sport so much.

They and others began to egg me on. I was hesitant at first because I would have to take off my clothes in front of everyone and change into the sumo belt. I finally agreed. Just as the ongoing match ended, one of the contestants was thrown off the clay ring onto his shoulder and head. He was knocked out. He couldn't lift his arm when he woke. Oh, God. Then I noticed the large young man who would be my opponent. What if he had a girlfriend in the audience and wanted to impress her by tossing me out on my ass...or head. I decided not to wrestle. To this day I regret the decision. It would have made a great family video and YouTube sensation.

Carpe Diem!

I had to wrestle the winner of this match. No thanks.

Everyone assumed I was Dr. Saario.

Alaskan Aleut scout Ted trying to figure out how to use a rod and reel.

GOING DOWN THE YUKON

Not A Five Star Trip

VERY FEW PEOPLE HAVE GONE all the way down the mighty Yukon River to the Bering Sea. I know why. It's over a thousand miles of mud, tundra, poverty and mosquitoes. I didn't know that when I agreed to go.

My old friend Edgar Hetteen from Arctic Enterprises knew I wanted to travel the great rivers of the world. When Arctic Cat decided to send two engineers down the Yukon to see why their outboard motors were plugging up with Yukon mud, Edgar elbowed his way into the trip. He talked me into going and without much time or research, I agreed. It was the trip from hell.

After loading two Silverline boats and one fishing boat powered by Spirit Outboards, we put in on the Tanana River south of Fairbanks. The Tanana flows into the Yukon and was the only pretty part of the trip. It was only about 100 miles long before it converged with the great Yukon.

I was happy Arctic had arranged for a guide so I could get some salmon fishing advice from him. I met Ted while he was trying to cast my spinning reel. Trying to cast? I asked Ted what was wrong. He said he had never used a rod and reel before and didn't know how to operate the bail system. A guide who didn't know how to fish?

We cast off on June 14th in a light rain with a 20 mph wind at around 50°. Our spirits were high. I found Ted to be a well-educated and interesting Aleut. He was hoping to see relatives about 500 miles downriver at the town of Russian Village. Ted told me that he had never been down the river before and was curious to see what it was like. And Ted was our guide!

About four hours into the trip we stopped at an abandoned native camp. It was a mess. Litter and junk everywhere. The branches were hung with black plastic sheeting flapping in the wind. It was the beginning of my feeling that the future of Alaska should not be left to Alaskans. I remembered going through residential Anchorage and noticing a stunning amount of debris and junk in every yard. I think the state's nomadic heritage affected all Alaskans. Make a mess and move on without cleaning it up.

As we moved into the swift-flowing waters of the Yukon we left the somewhat scenic Tanana and started our tour of almost 800 miles of tundra. Mud banks covered with six-foot bushes. We made camp in the mud on our first night and mud was with us for the remainder of the trip. Still, our spirits were high. I was the cook and we had adequate provisions to last us until we got to a native village along the way. On the second day we passed a large flat-bottomed boat. Little did we know it was the spring provisions barge. Virtually every village was out of everything except smoked and fresh salmon.

I learned there was no need for a rod and reel. If we needed a salmon we would power up to a fish wheel, reach into the live box and pull out a salmon.

Edgar was anxious to get to the first village to see if anyone recognized him from his precedent setting winter trip down the river twenty years ago. Edgar carried photos to show to various native families so they would not view him as a stranger. The first village came into view on day three. It was a joyous time for Edgar and a small family. We approached their small rough wooden home and worried about the many barking dogs. As we got closer the dogs would not let us get to the front door so we called out for the occupants. A man with a rifle came to the door and asked us what we wanted. Edgar said he was the man who came by snowmobile twenty years earlier and had stayed in this house overnight. Slowly other family members peered out the windows and door.

The man finally let us get close. Edgar showed the old photos to the man. He then realized Edgar was the snowmobile pioneer. He was overjoyed. The whole family was mesmerized by the photos. I don't think they had any pictures from that period and laughed and laughed at how they looked. The house was too small for all of us to go inside so the man brought us over to his smoked salmon stash and loaded us up with as much as we wanted. It was all hanging on ropes like laundry hanging on the line. Some of the salmon had been smoked but a lot of it was simply dried.

We had to climb down a mountain of garbage as we departed the village. The locals threw all their garbage and junk into the river. About an hour later we camped in the mud and had our fill of salmon both smoked and fresh grilled. The mosquitoes were especially bad. I also couldn't figure out what the white stuff on the other side of the river was, certainly not snow. Ted shook his head. We were in the middle of the first mosquito hatch.

The next night the mosquitoes swarmed and at times were as thick as clouds. We were shown how the malamutes protect their new litter of pups by placing the runt on top of the nest. The mosquitoes kill it by draining the pink-skinned pup of its blood saving the rest of the litter.

The first of five 40 horsepower motors silted up the next day. It took the engineers about two hours to get it running again as the rain got heavier. No sooner did we get the first one running and the second one went down. Another delay. If this continued, I knew we would not make the Bering Sea in eight more days.

We passed a few more garbage covered villages in the next few days and realized how badly they needed the supply barge to replenish their stores. Our plan to purchase necessary items along the way proved ill-conceived. The villagers were asking us for cooking oil, salt and above all else whiskey or beer.

I was in charge of cooking and rationing the beer supply. We now survived on powdered eggs and salmon. I prepared salmon in every way possible. Grilled, sautéed, poached, raw and fried. We always ate in the mud.

I rode with Ted in the 14' aluminum fishing boat while the others were in the larger cruisers. It was boring. Very boring. Each afternoon at four I would give everyone their first beer of the day. Ted became more talkative when he had a beer but after the second beer, he became angry, abusive and rather scary.

The same thing happened at the next stop. The third time I decided to film his change of behavior. It was amazing how his personality changed after only two beers. Thank God he couldn't have a third. I knew for certain Ted did not have any other alcohol. I had the only key to the beer chest. I'm sorry the constant rain ruined my film so I couldn't share this with interested parties.

On the seventh day we reached Russian Village and found a bottle of Jim Beam whiskey for sale for $100. We bought it and killed it that night passing the bottle around the campfire. We wouldn't let Ted imbibe which made him extremely angry. He refused to sleep in our canvas tents and went into the bush by himself.

The motors went down repeatedly from the silt. I had to leave the group at the village of St. Mary's and arrange for a bush pilot to take me to Anchorage. The pilot could only get me halfway but arranged to have another meet me and complete the trip. I had a slight financial problem. I didn't have enough cash to pay the pilots and only one check. "No problem. Just give it to the next guy. He'll take care of me when he gets it cashed in a few weeks."Alaskan bush pilots trust each other. Near the end of the trip from hell the Northwest Airlines DC-10s were grounded because of a huge mechanical problem. I ended up staying in an Anchorage hotel for three days until I got a seat on an Alaskan Airway flight to Vancouver, then to Seattle and home.

My three clearest memories. Mud, mosquitoes and Ted.

Sleeping in the open, yards away from big animals and mean chimps, required a lot of Ambien.

GREATEST TRIP

On To Zanzibar

TERRY AND I HAVE BEEN FORTUNATE to have traveled the world. Over 60 countries ranging from the extremes of Dogon Country in Mali, the desert of Mongolia, unwelcome in Algeria to a month with family in Ireland. Unfortunately, the most memorable trip for me was one that Terry had strange, foreboding feelings about so I went without her. Cancellation was impossible without paying for the entire, very elaborate trip.

David Bennett, my friend and lawyer, and members of his family had planned a trip to a remote part of Africa. We would follow Livingston's path from Arusha, to Lake Tanganyika, to the lower Selous Game Reserve, ending up in Zanzibar. It would be three long, rugged weeks with a lot of walking. It was guaranteed to be adventurous because very few have ever traveled the route.

Another friend of Dave's and mine, David Cox, bought Terry's part of the trip (thank God).

Our first camp was 40 miles south of Jan Goodall's camp on the shores of Lake Tanganyika. Our guide, his wife and new baby led the group. Our group consisted of Dave's wife, Sue, two cousins and their wives, David Cox and me. David Bennett's family were all experienced African travelers and knew how to put this unique trip together. They knew the top guide in Africa, Alan Crenshaw. He was the elected head of the Guides Association, a botanist, a biologist and a renaissance man.

We lived for the first four days in tents on the shore of the lake. Our mess tent was colorful and reminiscent of a Bedouin tent. Quite beautiful. The lake itself was amazing. 400 miles long sitting in the middle of Africa with water so pure we could eat the fish raw. We had sushi every night.

A camp a few miles away was occupied with two Japanese graduate students from Kyoto University and their wives. The University had been studying the lives of the chimps in the area since 1962. Every day the grad students filmed the chimps. They even constructed trails for the chimps to make it easier to find them.

The grad students, starved for social contact from the outside, were excited when I greeted them with my limited but perfectly accented Japanese. They were disappointed when they found my Japanese so limited.

Each day we hiked in the mountains and followed the activities of a troupe of about 40 chimps. We got to know their names and were able to identify them. We could come within two feet of them as they passed. We were instructed to never look them in the eyes as they would see that as an aggressive action and could bite.

Once Sue Bennett got too close to a baby. The mother climbed up onto a branch over Sue and emitted a brown liquid that hit Sue on the head and dirtied her shirt. I have an amazing video of the event. Sue begged us for our precious water to clean up. We gave her only enough to clean her face. At the end of the day she walked right into the lake without taking her clothes off.

Tanganyika is an amazingly clean lake, especially considering it borders Rwanda and Burundi. Both capital cities were built many miles away from the shore. There was virtually no water pollution and almost no villages on the hundreds of miles of shoreline. The natives seemed to build on rivers most likely for sanitation reasons.

A single-engine plane ferried us in two trips to a camp set up for us in a new national park in Tanzania. We were either the third or fourth group to ever go into this huge expanse of wilderness. As we landed, the plane took back four others who were leaving the camp. We all shook hands and said goodbye. Years later while having dinner with a couple in Hawaii Terry and I discovered they were the folks getting off the plane. It turned out that he was the co-author of *In Search of Excellence*, a bestselling business book.

This portion of the trip was to be a walking tour but we were confined to our vehicles for two days because a crocodile recently ate one of the staff who got too close to the riverbank fetching water. It would make very bad press if a tourist were lost this way. During the week in the park we saw only one other vehicle and six people. They were German oil engineers.

We saw many animal species and had our camp trampled by hippos (who eat at night). Our guide battled malaria for two days sweating it out in his tent.

The next week was spent in a more remote area in the lower Selous Game Reserve. We tracked black rhinos for five days to no avail. We found warm feces but failed to get a glimpse of this rare species.

On some nights we slept out in the open with only netting for protection. The beds were set up about thirty yards apart. At one point my bed was surrounded by three hyenas which scared the hell out of me. The night guard scared them away but they kept coming back. Looking back, sleeping out alone was one of the highlights of the trip.

We finished the trip on the island of Zanzibar. Our plane wasn't due until the next day so I had time to look around the exotic city. We were not allowed to take photos. I found a museum (the only one) and spent some time there. It was in terrible shape with rain coming through the roof. Anything metal in the building was rusted. Way back in a corner I saw some papers tacked to an accordion-like display. As I read the words I realized these papers were Stanley's notes from his famous book about Dr. Livingston. I was stunned and troubled by their condition and lack of care.

I almost drowned while swimming alone on our last night. I had never been in a riptide before and got caught in it as darkness fell. After almost a half-hour of panic, I realized I had to swim to shore at an angle to escape the riptide.

It was my greatest adventure. I am so sorry Terry was not with me but something bad might have happened if she had come along.

We will never know.

El Gaucho Gordo on a reluctant polo pony.

EL GAUCHO GORDO

The Fat Cowboy

WEIGHT HAS BEEN A PROBLEM for me the last 25 years. Terry and I were on a fancy estancia in Argentina when weight reared its ugly gut again.

The local gauchos wrapped a serape around my shoulders, put an Argentine beret on my large head and hoisted me on a fine Argentine pony. It was not a large horse but a beauty. But beauty did not want to move with me on his back. I can't blame him. I tried kicking with my heels, clicking with my lips, hollering "giddy up" but nothing worked. He was not going to move. Terry heard one of the cowboys say to the other, "El gaucho gordo." I'm forever branded el gaucho gordo, the fat cowboy.

I have lost ten pounds at least thirty times and gained ten pounds thirty-one times. That's a 600-pound exchange. I've tried many diets and remedies but the good old yoyo won out.

I went to Weight Watchers in 2008. It was a doozy. The instructor was brand new and this was my maiden voyage. The other four in the class were regulars. A geeky guy used the meetings as his total social outlet talking about all the things he avoided eating the past week. He was so proud of himself. The other three women attended together, all sentenced by their employer, Allina Health, to lose weight. Then there was Miss Giggly, the instructor, a severe Nurse Ratched look-alike.

The small room was immediately adjacent to the YMCA basketball court. The door that faced the court couldn't close so our class was interrupted with the thump of the ball, the boing of the rim and the slaps and grunts of the players five feet from our meeting room door.

I knew this was going to be my last meeting when Miss Giggly started her presentation with cards starting with the letter "I" as in inspiration. At least I got the famed Weight Watchers point system book. I had tried to buy it at Barnes and Noble but it's only sold at WW meetings. Ugh!

Then the next day I left the water running in the kitchen sink and it overflowed. My coveted book on the counter was now water-logged. I am not going back for another.

Definitely not a polo pony.

The faint outline of a woman and the imprint of a foot directing the sailors to the prostitutes before entering the city of Ephesus. Could be one of the world's first ads.

EPHESUS

The World's First Advertisement

THE ANCIENT LIBRARY AT EPHESUS is one of the most heavily visited tourist sites in Turkey. It was our good luck to visit on a rainy day in November when only one other person was there.

The sun surprisingly broke through the overcast sky and made the marble library even more beautiful. Because we were alone I laid down on the marble terrace looking up at the façade. I fell asleep while Terry explored.

She interrupted my snooze with exciting news. An ad was carved into a stone walkway. History's first advertisement. A woman's head and a finger pointing to the left followed by a footprint.

This image greeted sailors getting off their Mediterranean ships, telling them not to come into town without first visiting the baths and the waiting prostitutes.

Advertising with a purpose.

Remote part of Mali.

DOGON COUNTRY

A Dangerous Trip

TRAVELING THROUGH WEST AFRICA for three weeks with only a driver, a guide and our two friends, Marie-Noëlle and Fred Meyer, was the way to see Africa.

On our way to Dogon Country we stopped to observe a ritual puberty dance in an isolated village. The four of us were the only non-Africans in the village. Drums provided the beat and fermented corn the liquor. Lots of liquor. Everyone seemed drunk. Marie-Noëlle and Terry were pressured into dancing with older women in the tribe. Terry really got into it while Marie-Noëlle was traumatized. We sensed this could get out of control so we made for the truck. Whew!

After a couple hours traveling on dirt roads we descended into Dogon Country. We sensed it may be dangerous when we were told to sign in as we crossed the border so the authorities would know when we came out. There were warning signs advising us to stay on the road and not to venture into the bush. Cannibalism was still active in Dogon Country.

We went under a natural bridge as we entered a small village. The smell was overwhelming. People were filling their cups with blood as a goat was being bled. We were not invited to join them...thank goodness. Elsewhere women were pounding massive raw onions with large paddles. The desiccated onions were then rolled into compact balls and left on large flat rocks to dry. This was a staple in their diet and a means for trade.

The village was on the edge of a 1000-foot sheer wall and we could see the plain below for miles. The Dogon people buried their dead in the cliff walls by lowering the corpse with ropes and inserting the body into a small cave.

No one seemed friendly and we were relieved to leave. As we drove away we saw a circular building off in the distance. We were told that this is where women stay during menstruation. I called the building "period architecture."

A few hours later we stopped at the only source for gasoline, a 55-gallon drum located outside a shanty. Terry heard voices singing Christmas carols in English from the back of the shanty. Tourists rarely came to this part of Africa. Four Peace Corp workers had come from miles around to share the Christmas spirit. We surprised them. They were excited to get news from the States and loved Terry's t-shirt with the front page of the *Minneapolis Star Tribune* printed on it. They were intent reading about the Minnesota Twins victory in the World Series. Terry gave them the shirt.

We experienced West Africa as few have.

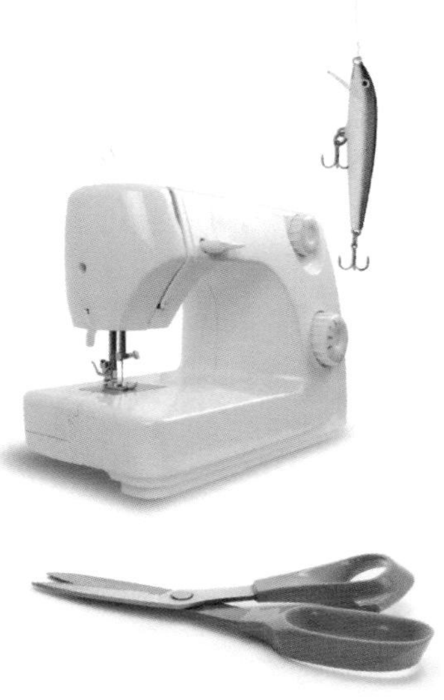

ASLEEP IN FINLAND

While Standing Up

My friend and great art director Jim Lotter traveled with me to visit three clients in Scandinavia–Rapala Lures and Knives, Viking Sewing Machines and Fiskars Scissors.

The trip was a lark but a good idea to show our interest in their business. Because we were not experienced European travelers our schedule left much to be desired. We tried to cover all three locations in six days not knowing it was a five-hour drive from Helsinki to the Rapala factory in northern Finland.

We started with a plant tour in Husqvarna, Sweden. Inflation was raging at 14% all over Europe and the US. It was the main topic of conversation. I learned how to say, "Inflation is causing sales problems" in both Swedish and Finnish. The plant tour was boring as usual but what interested me was not on the agenda.

To improve efficiency they put great emphasis on starting meetings precisely on time and were testing some radical ideas. For example, if you were late to the meeting the door would be closed. You were admonished by a sign on the door stating you apparently thought you were more important than this meeting starting on time.

A couple interesting ideas emerged from the meeting. A stone was placed in front of you if you were in charge of the meeting. If a boss tried to take over or talk too much you would move the stone over to the boss. They also had a 90 minute clock hand on a whiteboard. The agenda was put on the board to show how much time you had for each subject. The clock hand moved past the items as they were discussed. If you could not finish in the allotted time the item was moved to a wing of the board and assigned to a later meeting. On the other wing were the actions or decisions made during that segment. I tried it at Carmichael Lynch. Rebellion.

They also had a group of rooms for standing meetings, no chairs. You had to use the standing rooms if you didn't have an agenda and the meeting could not go beyond 15 minutes.

Our first meeting in Finland was with Fiskars in Helsinki. They were very cool to us and assigned a person to take us out for drinks. The bar was austere but high end. White walls with no art, acrylic furniture and bland carpeting. The waiter came over with a bottle of scotch and placed it on the table along with the glasses. We were charged by a measurement of the bottle. We drank way too much trying to liven up our host. He stayed sober, we did not. Jet lag was starting to consume us. We had a terrible time staying awake. We went to our hotel rooms and slept for only a few hours when we were awakened by the hotel and told our car and driver were ready to leave for northern Finland and the Rapala factory.

We climbed into a plush Mercedes and instantly fell asleep. It was a warm fall afternoon with the sun reflecting off the snow. The curving roads kept us sound asleep until the car stopped at some type of event. We saw many people standing on the front steps of the building clapping their hands. Our driver, who spoke English, was to be our interpreter. He said the clapping was for us. We were surprised and tried to comb our hair and tuck in our shirts. We looked hungover. One of the Rapala brothers read a proclamation honoring Carmichael Lynch. Our advertising was so effective they could now employ the 200 gathered factory workers. The event was for us.

We were led inside to begin a long tour and then ushered into a very warm conference room where the three Rapala brothers waxed on and on about inflation and their fears. They wanted to know what we were going to do about it. It went on forever because the interpreter was not too swift. As the sun lowered in the sky it came right into the conference room window heating the room further and making Jim and me deadly drowsy. Jim finally had to stand up to prevent falling asleep in the chair. About five minutes later I heard a loud crash. I turned and saw a large trophy and product case shattered with glass all over the floor. Jim was bright red. It seemed he had fallen asleep on his feet and fallen back against the case. Ouch.

The Rapala brothers took us to a real Finnish sauna as a special treat. It was located on a lake with a trapdoor in the floor covering the mushy ice water below. We got hot and were whipped (I mean whipped) with branches. When we were red enough, we all had to jump into the hole, swim underwater back to the ladder and start all over again. I could not do it again. They thought we were both "punies."

That night the Rapala brothers took us to the only night club in the region and fed us cloudberry wine, a local specialty. It was ghastly. The noise from the band was deafening and the translator was too bored to help us communicate, leaving me with the only thing I could say in Finnish. "Inflation sure is bad."

And so was the trip.

Trying, with no success, to get the donkey to cross the Salmon River via the only bridge within many miles.

RIVER NOSE

The Burro Lift

ONE OF MY EARLY GOALS IN LIFE was to run the great rivers of the world. I have been on the Thames, Seine, Mekong, Danube, Yangtze, Nile and many of the important rivers in the US.

I planned a trip down the Amazon that was to start with a hiking trek and a whitewater week in Peru. The trip was canceled. I went to the Aspen Institute instead. You know what happened there. I met Terry Saario. Glad the Amazon trip was canceled but I still hope to go there someday.

Doug Hart, a former Green Bay Packer, Ed McKie, Ed Michalek and I went on a one-week trip down the Middle Fork of the Salmon River in Idaho. We were with a group of ten men who were all kayakers. Ed McKie and Doug had kayaked before and urged me to take some lessons. Since it was winter I had to take lessons in a swimming pool. I used the pool at the Decathlon Club and became adept at doing the Eskimo roll and other escape maneuvers.

We flew to Boise and met up with our group after a long bumpy school bus ride to the "put in" area. Mr. Mason, our leader, gave us final safety instructions and told us if we were uncomfortable shooting some of the more difficult rapids we could ride on the supply raft or paddle in the four-man inflatable. I felt ready for the rapids in a kayak. Why not?

Within one hour after putting in we hit the first of many rapids. It was a grade two on a five-point scale. A five was a killer and we would need to be roped down. The grading of rapids changes throughout the season based on water flow. Sometimes a grade one could become three or four even if the water flow was lower and slower.

As the first rapids approached I found my adrenalin rising. From a hundred feet away the rapids looked gigantic and this one had only a rating of two. I got a real rush as we entered the shoot. At the first turn I flipped and found my head bouncing on the bottom of the river. The water was frigid. Then my face smashed against a rock because I was underwater facing downriver. It almost knocked me out. By the time we all assembled at the calm pool below the rapids, I was pumping blood out of my smashed nose. Thank goodness I didn't lose any teeth and was wearing a helmet. My nose felt broken.

I found out quickly that doing an Eskimo roll in a swimming pool was not the equivalent of doing one in two feet of cold water at 10 mph.

I plugged my nose with cotton and climbed aboard the supply raft for the remainder of the day. I sat there with the guide, the cook and two older women, breathing through my mouth holding my throbbing head.

That night sleeping on a thin mat on the ground was almost impossible because every time I turned over, I hit my nose and it started to bleed again. By breakfast I had stopped the flow and agreed to paddle in the four-man inflatable.

About midday after a few more level two rapids, Ed McKie decided to join me in the raft because a couple of level four rapids were coming up soon. Ed was in front of me and loved the rush of the moment when the tip of the raft dug into the foam. A big one sent Ed flying in the air right over me.

As he flayed about, his knee hit me directly in...you guessed it... my nose. My eyes water just thinking about the pain. My black and blue bruised face was once again covered with blood.

Back to the supply raft. That night I hardly slept but by the next morning I was ready to go back to the four-man raft.

The scenery was beautiful and remote. Once you start down the Salmon there is no going back. On the fourth day we went under the first of only two bridges over the river. We were frantically hailed by someone high above us on the shore.

A wilderness hiker had lost half of his supplies and all of his cooking gear when one of his two donkeys fell over the cliff and was washed down the river. He desperately needed to get to the other side of the river with his donkey but the animal wouldn't go on the narrow bridge. If he could cross the river he could get back to civilization in two days instead of three weeks if he had to follow his original plan.

We thought that if we covered the animal's eyes and tightly grabbed and held his legs, we could carry him over the bridge. I held the rear left leg, Ed, Ed, and Doug held the other legs. The hiker covered the donkey's head with a towel. Although the animal weighed only about 150 lbs. it was 150 lbs. of muscle. It was a struggle to hold on as it attempted to kick us. It was lucky no one got hurt, including the animal. What a stupid idea!

Defeated, we gave the poor hiker a few candy bars, gum and cigarettes and wished him well.

I don't know how he got back or if he got back at all.

The Swedish delegation pitching Ostersund, Sweden for the Winter Olympic Games. Atlanta had 500 delegates doing the same thing.

SWEDISH OLYMPICS

A Japanese TV *Star*

TERRY AND I HAPPENED TO BE IN TOKYO at the same time as our dear friends from Sweden Bob and Christina Persson. We had a lovely dinner at a shabu-shabu restaurant. Bob revealed that they, along with his cousin and wife, were the Swedish delegation for Sweden's bid for the winter Olympics in their hometown, Ostersund, Sweden.

Ostersund's government thought they did not have much of a chance in the bidding and thus sent only the four of them. Atlanta and Nagano, Japan were the most likely winners in the contest for the summer Olympics. Atlanta sent 500 delegates.

That evening while we were dining, some dramatic changes occurred in Sweden's chances to get the winter games. Atlanta won the summer games, thereby eliminating Salt Lake City from contention for the winter games. Moscow pulled out because of political instability and Barcelona pulled out because of money. Suddenly Ostersund was left in the winter competition with only one other city, Nagano.

After Bob found out about the changes in Ostersund's prospects, he called me at I-house (International House in Roppongi) and asked, "Lee, do you have a suit?" I said I did. He said come over to our hotel right away and be Swedish. I didn't know what that meant but I hustled over and met him. He explained that his cousin and he and Christina had media interviews and couldn't be in their suite to give out brochures and information about Ostersund. Everyone wanted to know where the heck Ostersund was and what was it like.

Bob and Christina left for an important interview with NKH, the national Japanese TV station. Somehow in the muddy translations between Swedish, Japanese and English, the television journalists confused the place for the interview. It was not to be at the station but in the hotel.

While I expected to sit in the room and pass out brochures, I ended up having to deal with a camera crew from NKH. I wasn't sure what to do. I greeted them in Japanese and then switched to one of the few phrases I knew in Swedish. They said they didn't speak Swedish so was it possible to conduct the interview in English? "Engrish," I said. "Yah, Engrish would be good."

There I was being interviewed in English while claiming to be Swedish before some Japanese reporters. Thank God they didn't catch on.

Since I had been to Ostersund, I could answer their rhetorical questions with a simple yes or no. "Was Ostersund beautiful?" they asked.

"Yah, Ostersund is very beautiful," I replied. And on it went.

That night I was on Japanese TV posing as a Swede. Unfortunately, the station did not save the interview, so it was lost to posterity.

As a finalist, Ostersund was host to the Olympic search committee. The town and my friends put their best foot forward. Only one problem. The King of Sweden forgot to put the date of the event on his calendar and was not present to host his own party for the committee. An embarrassing disaster for Sweden and the King.

Nagano was awarded the games.

From Beijing to Moscow on the Istanbul Nostalgic Orient Express.

SIBERIAN SPRINT

A Dangerous Race

YEARS AGO TERRY AND I TOOK the Trans-Siberian Nostalgic Oriental Express train from Beijing to Moscow. We were hooked when we saw the travel brochure. Eleven days on a train to some of the most remote parts of the world.

The passengers were an interesting lot. We were all up for an unusual adventure.

The train was not as luxurious as it claimed. It was built in Eastern Germany in 1952 and needed more than cosmetic upgrades even though the Lalique glass insets throughout the train were original. Overstuffed chairs in the dining car looked comfortable but lacked springs and the seats fell almost to the floor. The cabins were tiny and only one person could dress at a time. Food was quite basic–lots of potatoes, boiled eggs and leathery meat that smelled like dog. But the vodka flowed.

Large, stern Mongolian guards entered the train as we transferred from Chinese control into Mongolia. Not a single smile as they checked our passports. The border town was a tiny, dusty place in the middle of nowhere, with the strange distinction of having several blocks in the town's streets filled with pool tables. Several passengers from the train strolled into town to buy water only to discover the bottles were used and not sterile. Children ran around without diapers and used the ground as their toilet facility.

The train ran at night giving us time to tour and explore during the day. Every stop was well planned and quite informative.

One late night in the dining car we were treated to the most miraculous sight. Hundreds of wild Mongolian horses playfully ran alongside the train bathed in moonlight. It seemed to be a game for them. It was stunningly beautiful.

Mongolia was a treat. As the train pulled into Ulan Bator, we noticed an old, grey Chevrolet speeding alongside. In it was the US Consul, late for our arrival, putting on his tie while rushing to greet the honored guest aboard, General William Westmoreland.

General Westmoreland was the highest-ranking military person to have ever visited Mongolia. As we departed the train, a Mongolian mounted drill squad performed some of the most intricate maneuvers I could ever imagine.

We were escorted out to the Mongolian tundra where we drank fermented horse milk, dined in a yurt and rode the famous Mongolian ponies. I was thrown in about thirty seconds and chose not to remount. Earlier in Ulan Bator, we enjoyed a Mongolian performance with dance and throat singing.

We visited the world's largest body of freshwater, Lake Baikal, which is drinkable without being treated with chemicals. While trudging through the mud (there was mud everywhere) I greeted a local with my limited Russian. "Dobre utro!" He replied in English, "Where are you from?" I replied, "Minnesota." He was at Lake Baikal as part of a University of Minnesota water research project. Small world.

Every stop gave us an insight into Russian culture. The last day was a long one. The train ran for twenty hours straight non-stop through the most boring part of the famous Russian tundra.

The train had to make one stop to stock up on water—both potable and for the showers. We were told that under no circumstance were we to get off the train.

Of course, I got off to stretch my legs. Terry did not know that I had left the train. I was standing on a concrete platform about ten feet wide and one hundred feet long when the train started to move. My car was ahead of me so I tried to board on the next one except its gate was closed.

Electric trains today are not the chug, chug slow to start monsters of old. This one was like a Tesla...quick to take off and pick up speed.

The gate on the next car was also closed. My jogging became a slow run. When the exit on the next car was also closed I started to panic. I had to sprint and was running out of platform.

Thank God the gate to the next and last car was open. I had to grab on and hoist my body up onto the step without using my legs.

Only after I calmed down and thought about the risk I'd taken did I realize how stupid I was. No hat. Ninety degrees. No water or food. No passport or identification. Out in the middle of nowhere. Mosquito swarms would be coming at dusk and no trains were scheduled for hours. And nothing as far as the eye could see, nothing but flat tundra.

I hope my kids don't do stupid things.

To pass the time on the train, Terry and I decided to create our own plot for a *Murder on the Orient Express.* A man had been found in the bar car with a knife in his back. Who did it? I interviewed everyone on the train and had them come up with alibis. Everyone participated except the General and his wife.

At the closing banquet in Moscow, I introduced the four candidates who were the most likely suspects. Our fellow travelers voted on who was the villain. Raucous cheers rang out for one suspect or another but no one voted for poor old, nearly blind Albert, the 91 year-old former banker who was accompanied by a 40ish "hottie" photographer. But Albert was the villain. He did it. The deceased had hit on his "hottie" and Albert took revenge. Early in the train trip the "hottie" offloaded responsibility for Albert onto Terry and me.

We classified some of the older travelers on the train into one of three categories: the "fallers," the "pushers" and the "whaters." Albert, because of his visual issues, tended to fall frequently. Those grossly overweight or severely inflexible had to be pushed up onto the first step to the rail car. The "whaters" couldn't hear well and kept saying "what?"

Now, 25 years later Terry and I probably fit into one of those categories. Not so funny now.

OBITUARY

Wisdom For The Ages

LELAND T. LYNCH OBITUARY

Written March 2022

Tom and Ethel Lynch of Belle Plaine, Minnesota, told their son Lee that everyone will eventually die of shortness of breath (their joke). Lee did just that on xxxx. He died. Checked out, croaked, or as they used to say in Belle Plaine, "he was taken under."

It wasn't a valiant death. He didn't fight it, he tried to run from it but got caught and was put into the arms of his cremator.

He lived a lucky life:

– *Had the great advantage of being born in a small town.*

– *Went to a great university when the annual tuition was $180.*

– *Was in a favorable age cohort.*

– *Lucky to have succeeded in a business he started without knowing anything about advertising.*

– *Had three great children (Molly, Chris and Kate), perfect in-laws, nine grandkids, two great grands and a few extended family members.*

– *Started a lot of things that succeeded and some that did not.*

– *A passionate Democrat who shook the hand of every democratic candidate for president, from Hubert Humphrey to Joe Biden.*

– *Had a love affair with the State of Minnesota which caused him to write a book, Amazing MN.*

– *But his greatest love affair was with his beautiful wife of forty years, Dr. Terry Saario.*

Everyone and anyone are encouraged to attend his
memorial service, a fundraiser ($25 minimum) for the
environmental organization, *Earthjustice.*
State Theatre, 805 Hennepin, Minneapolis, MN
Program at 3:30 p.m. Cocktails at 5 p.m.
Call Rosanne for details.

That's all there is. Thanks for reading.